A Stroke of Love

The Story Of One Couple's Journey Through A Stroke

By

DARLENE CHISSOM

A Story about overcoming the tragic effects of a catastrophic stroke. One couple's journey helping each other deal with the loss of their life as they knew it.

authorHOUSE

AuthorHouse™
1663 Liberty Drive
Bloomington, IN 47403
www.authorhouse.com
Phone: 1 (800) 839-8640

Published by AuthorHouse 01/08/2018

ISBN: 978-1-5246-4527-4 (sc)
ISBN: 978-1-5246-4525-0 (hc)
ISBN: 978-1-5246-4526-7 (e)

Library of Congress Control Number: 2016917034

Print information available on the last page.

For Phill

You are my yesterday, my today, and my tomorrow

I Love You

Acknowledgments

I had so much help in writing this book. The task seemed quite daunting at first. In a year where I had trouble putting simple thoughts together, let alone sentences, and paragraphs, God lent me a hand. He helped me to find the right words to express our feelings, and tell our story. We serve an awesome God!

I would like to extend so many thanks to Huck and Marcia Heintz for their help in writing this book. Your input helped make it, what it is.

To my friend, and fellow Christian, Tracy, thank you for praying for this to be a guide for others, and for the countless sticky notes, I found throughout the book. You have no idea how much you made Phill laugh. For that alone, I love you!

Farming is a 24/7 365 commitment. Your day is spent, doing what is necessary to keep animals fed, and taken care of, crops grown, and harvested, buildings, and machinery in repair. Ignore one of these, and all will fail.

This pretty much describes farming. My husband was born on this farm over 70 years ago. His father before him farmed this land, and milked cows. This has been my husband's life, all of his life. Phill carried a milker practically, since he was old enough to walk. He has worked from before the sun rises, to well after it sets, sometimes, even through the night, to get the work done, that needs to be done. This is more than his life, it has been his love.

On average every 40 seconds, someone has a stroke. According to **strokecenter.org,** there are 795,000 people who will have a stroke in the US this year. Will it be you? Or someone you love? Will it strike today, or tomorrow? You have no way of knowing, until it happens. You will be living your life, going on about your business, when your life as you know it, is left in shambles. Your livelihood, your future, even the love of your life, has changed. "A Stroke of Love" gives you a day to day account, from the day my husband suffered a devastating stroke, through his first year of recuperation. It was not an easy journey. We now faced the loss of our dairy, we had built in our thirty years together. A farm handed down, from father to son. We had to deal with thoughts of suicide, despair, and desolation. We learned how to pick up the pieces, and begin to build a new life.

Chapter 1

I find the rhythmic beeping of the monitors above Phill's bed to be comforting in an uneasy way. That constant sound means my husband is still breathing, and his heart is still beating. I watch him lying there sleeping, and think how peaceful he looks. You would never guess by watching him, the battle going on inside his brain. His chest rises and falls in a systematic pattern, and his eyes flutter like he is dreaming. I wonder if he is dreaming.

Even with the glass doors closed, I can hear the bustling sounds of the ICU. Nurses, doctors, and families quietly move up and down the hall like a living, breathing organism. I close my eyes and repeat the prayer that I have been saying all day: "Please, God, let him live." My mind has a hard time understanding how this could have happened. Nothing has prepared me for this morning. When I look back now, I try to remember when I awoke this morning if I had a sense of foreboding, or dread, or even a feeling that something was wrong. I can't remember feeling anything out of the ordinary. It seemed to be a morning just like every other morning. I woke up, and got out of bed. Phill, my husband, was already up. I could hear the TV downstairs in the basement, and him taking care of the woodstove. I went to the kitchen, fixed my coffee, turned the fireplace on, and sat on the couch to start my day. Just another ordinary day. Or so I thought.

Day 1: Six Hours Earlier

My husband, and I have a daily routine. Since my elderly parents had moved in almost four years ago, we have our private time to talk first thing in the morning. I usually sit in the living room in the dark, and drink my coffee. My husband has already been up for an hour or two, had his breakfast, and watched the news. Phill usually tells me funny or informative things he has watched on his programs. All of that changed in a matter of seconds on April 9, 2015. It started out the same as every other day. We were sitting in the living room in the dark, I was drinking my coffee, and he was telling me a story. All at once, Phill's speech has began to slur. His words ran together in a garbled clutter of syllables. After spending almost thirty-one years with this man I was very aware of his speech patterns. I immediately asked him, "What is the matter?" His response was, "Iownknow." I jumped up to turn on a light, and got my first real look at Phill. I noticed the odd angle he held his head. It was turned slightly to the left with the top of his head cocked to the right. He was looking up to the left, out in space, as if listening for something that only he could hear. Phill then tried to get out of a chair, which he normally has no trouble rising from. It took him five tries to accomplish this. He wandered to the kitchen, his gait was unsteady. He headed for the cupboard where he kept his pills. Once there, he was unsure which one it was and reached in midair, groping for something that only he could see. Seeing that he had no idea of what he was doing, I grabbed a chair, and said, "Sit down!" I stood on his left side, holding his arm. He didn't even know I was there. I moved further in front of him, and more forcefully said, "YOU SIT DOWN!" He sat down. Phill wanted his blood pressure pills so I allowed him to take them, along with a baby aspirin. I also gave him another baby aspirin. I dialed Young Phill, our oldest son, and told him he needed to get up here because something was wrong with Dad.

I called 911, and told the operator that we needed an ambulance, because I thought my husband, was having a stroke. By then, Phill decided, he needed to go to the bathroom, so I helped him in there. The 911 operator had me do some basic tests for stroke. She had me ask him to smile; the left side of his face didn't move. She then had me tell him to raise both arms above his head. His left was slightly lower, and could not stay at that height, it began dropping. Then he had to recite a phrase, and you could hear the slurring of his words. The ambulance was dispatched. We were about to learn that

2

at approximately 6:45 a.m., my husband suffered, as far as we know his first period of A-Fib, (Atrial Fibrillation). That is when the top part of the heart, instead of beating its normal pattern, quivers. The blood that was in the top chamber formed a clot. When the heart resumed its normal beat, it sent that clot directly to the right side of Phill's brain, causing a stroke. That tiny blood clot, now was creating a potentially life-threatening brain injury for Phill. The longer it went without treatment, the more devastation it would leave in its wake.

At this point Young Phill arrived, I had him stay in the bathroom with his dad while I threw on some clothes, before the ambulance got here. I also called a friend who had helped us in the past, to see if he could milk the cows, and take care of the chores. By the time I finished, the ambulance had arrived. The EMTs took his vitals, and asked if anyone had told us, that he had an irregular heartbeat. "No," Phill, and I, both replied, he had never been diagnosed with an irregular heartbeat.

I have to take a minute to include a few minor details. My mom had just gotten up. My dad passed away the previous October from kidney failure. I also had three of our grandchildren, who were on break from school, staying with us. They had just arrived the day before. Mom, and three young children, watched these events unfold. Mom had not been well, since dad had died. I was afraid that she, and the kids would be so scared. I tried to assure them, their Big Pa would be just fine. Inside, I wasn't so sure.

While waiting for the ambulance to leave the driveway I began calling the other kids, and family. We are a blended family. Young Phill, Brian, and our oldest daughter Jenny are from Phill's first marriage, the two younger girls, Tamy, and Jamie, are mine from a previous marriage. Jenny left immediately for the hospital, and Brian would not be far behind. Young Phill had to take a few minutes to take care of some things at his coal business, our middle daughter, Tamy lives in Buffalo. She would be a couple of hours, and our youngest, Jamie lives in Laramie, Wyoming. She would only be able to talk on the phone with us. However, both of our youngest children were nurses, and that would prove to be a blessing. I also needed to call Phill's sister in Maine. This was a particularly hard call, as just five days ago, Beva's husband, had suffered two heart attacks in one day. I knew this would be very hard on her.

My mind raced all the way to the hospital. My thoughts focused on the obvious questions. How serious was this? Will he live? My hands were shaking on the wheel, and I felt sweaty, yet cold at the same time. I was scared. The hospital was at least twenty-five miles from our home, which provided a lot of thinking time. Brian called me, he was a few miles behind me on the interstate. As I pulled into the hospital, I saw Jenny waiting in the parking lot. I hurried over to the ambulance bay, and she joined me. As they opened the doors, and started to unload him, I asked how he was doing. I guess I hoped, his condition had improved. I knew that sometimes strokes could be very mild, and you recovered in a matter of minutes. They are called TIAs (Transient Ischemic Attacks) or, mini strokes. This hope was quickly dashed by the paramedic, who told me, there had been no change. By now Young Phill, and Brian had arrived. We filed in line behind the gurney, as they wheeled Phill in. As soon as we got in our room, the room was immediately teaming with people. There were doctors, nurses, and techs who helped to get him undressed, and into a gown. Monitors were connected, blood drawn. It was like a special dance where everyone knew their places, and their steps… except us. We just stood there, and watched. The doctor assessed, how much was affected by the stroke. Phill could read, and recognize words. That was good. He could talk, but with significant slurring. He could raise his left arm, although it couldn't maintain the height he raised it to. He was able to move his left leg, but not as well as his right. So far, it didn't look too bad. That was when we discovered he had, what they called, left-sided neglect. You could stand close to him on his left side, and he could not hear, or see you. You could touch his left arm or leg, and he could not feel your touch.

4

He had no idea you were there. Walk a few feet around in front of him, and he immediately responded. It was weird. They sent him for a CT scan to check for brain bleeds. This was another cause of a stroke. He did not have a bleed. We were told that he qualified for a shot of TPA, which is short, for Tissue Plasminogen Activator. A drug, which thins the blood, to the point, that it stops the clot from causing further damage. They would have to send him to the ICU to monitor. With this drug, there was a chance he could bleed to death from a minor injury, or the stroke itself. If we didn't give him the shot, then the blood clot, which caused the stroke, would continue to cause trauma in Phill's brain. It could eventually cause death, or permanent disabilities, which may be so severe, that he wouldn't be able to recover from it. The kids, and I made the decision together. We chose for Phill, to have a shot at life, with the TPA. We prayed our choice was the right one. They initially graded him a four, on the stroke scale, which was relatively low, on the National Institutes of Health Stroke Scale. Young Phill brought me food, and coffee. I drank the coffee, but the fear that I felt, rendered me unable to eat the bagel. It felt like I had a huge ball in the pit of my stomach. I decided to wait on eating. The ER staff packaged him up, and we headed to ICU.

When we arrived, we were greeted by our ICU nurse. Her name was Renni. I was surprised; she was one of my clients. I have been a photographer for over twenty years, and had, photographed her children on several occasions. It was great to see a familiar face. Renni explained, what we could expect to happen, as the day wore on. She told us they expected his stroke numbers to initially rise, but then they should come down, and stay there. They really didn't want his number to fluctuate. That would indicate a larger event. We sat around for most of the day, watching him sleep, and waiting. Every few minutes they came in, and assessed his condition. I took walks in the hall, and answered calls from friends, and family members. One of these calls, was my sister in Wyoming. Six days earlier, she had a catastrophic accident, in her pickup. She had been airlifted to the nearest trauma center, with a multitude of very serious injuries. In the days following her wreck, I struggled deeply with whether or not to fly to Wyoming. I decided, as long as her condition remained stable, I would not go. I felt in my heart, I wasn't supposed to go. The reason, now was abundantly clear. Had I gone, I would not have been here with Phill, when he had his stroke. No one would have. The chance that he may not have made it, or suffered damage beyond repair, were great. Though, heavily sedated, the nurse in my sister kicked in, she asked questions about Phill's condition. It seemed good to hear her interrogating me, instead of the drugged responses, that I was used to, since her accident. The rest of the day I cried. I worried. I paced. Phill slept on. Renni explained, this was normal for stroke patients. They need sleep.

The kids went to get some lunch. I stayed with Phill, I just couldn't leave. He seemed so vulnerable, laying there. I was afraid if I left, so would he…forever. So I stayed, and I prayed. God, and I had some very long talks in the first few days. I watched, and waited. I guess I thought, the TPA was such a miracle drug, he would return to normal, that very day, right before my eyes. His condition remained unchanged. I noticed his left side showed considerably more weakness, than it had in the ER. Phill's stroke scale number had now climbed to eight where it remained. It did not fluctuate, but it did not go back down either.

Brian, and I spent the night in the ICU with Phill. The nurses came in every fifteen minutes to do assessments. I dreaded those visits. I kept listening, watching for the things he couldn't do. I watched as he tried without success to raise his left arm, and left leg. I listened to every response he made to every question, waiting for the wrong answer. The stress of these visits, making me sick. Finally, at one a.m. we stayed up, and drank coffee. We watched the man we loved, trying to sleep between visits from the nurses. Finally, the world outside began to lighten. We had survived our first night in the ICU. This was Brian's last night to stay. I insisted he go home. I would watch over his dad for him. I knew it was a hard decision for him.

Chapter 2

Day 2

Day two in the ICU had begun. Phill was the same. Left side was still not working. The kids were back. All of them were present, except Jamie. She wanted to come so bad. Her dad was adamant, that she NOT come. She, and her daughter, had just moved into an apartment, financially, it would have been a strain. Renni came, and told us they were taking Phill, for an MRI, to check the damage done by the stroke. They had to wait twenty-four hours, after the shot of TPA, before they could do an MRI. Renni assured us, she would remain with Phill. She was not allowed to leave him. We remained in his room. When they returned, Renni immediately left to make a phone call. Her face told us, there was a problem. When she was off the phone, the boys, and I, went to the desk. I said, "He has a brain bleed doesn't he?" She replied, "No, why do you ask?" "I see by your face, there is something wrong," I said to her. She then told us, she had called in the hospital's Stroke Specialist. He was the, "go to" guy, who figured out, what no one else could. When the specialist looked at the MRI, he could not believe, Phill was still able to, somewhat walk, and talk. Rennie, and I, had been able to get him out of bed, and to the bathroom, that morning. It was not pretty, but we were able to accomplish getting him there, and back. The Specialist said, he should not have been able to do that with the damage to his brain. Nobody told my wonderful husband that. This was who he is. A doer!

Day 3

Our second night came, and went. Every time Phill needed to go to the bathroom, I got up, and helped the nurse. I sat there with him, just to be with him. Time, I found, is a very precious thing.

7

They brought him food today. He ate just a few bites then forgot what he was doing. He was more interested in talking to whomever was there, and so distracted, he was unable to eat. I encouraged him, and he would say, "Ok, I'll eat," and immediately go back to talking. My usually focused husband, could not stay on the simplest of tasks. Not even eating. He ended up losing seventeen pounds in the hospital. He was very emotional, and cried often. Through his tears, he told every one of us, how much he loved us. He no longer could remember conversations that had taken place minutes before, or who had been there to see him.

One day bled into another. I hadn't left the hospital since we came in. Jenny brought me clothes, and I washed up in the bathroom. One of the nurses, pulled some strings, and sent me to one of the floors, for a much needed shower. It was heavenly to just stand there in the hot water. We had been in the ICU three days. Three very long days.

When I got back to the floor, PT had come to walk Phill. The first lap around the nurse's station, he successfully walked two grown men, into both sides of the walls, in all four sections. He was all over the place, and could not stand without assistance. This was so hard to watch. I have always told Phill that he walks like a little Banty Rooster, proud, and with purpose. His once strong legs, were now filled with jelly. Nothing worked right. I had to do something. The second lap, I walked backwards in front of him, teasing him. I told him to catch me. We made eye contact. His posture straightened. He began to walk towards me, in a straight line. Maybe not perfect, but darn close. As long as he looked at me, he was focused. He was laughing, as we made the trek around the hall. The difference in his gait, was night, and day. He still needed a lot of assistance, but he was not bouncing off the walls. That was progress. It was decided, two people could walk him; one in front holding is hands, making him maintain eye contact, and the other, walking behind, steadying him, with their hands on his hips. It worked. We had a plan.

Chapter 3

Day 4

Phill moved out of ICU, and to a regular room on the floor. Friends who couldn't visit before, could now stop by. My brother brought my mom, who hadn't seen Phill since the morning of his stroke. She was glad to see him. Other friends stopped in, to chat. He was very animated, almost childlike, in his happiness.

He was still unable to raise his left arm, or leg, on command. Nothing, seemed to be working, on his left side. With that said, Brian called, he needed to grind feed for the cows. I noticed, while Phill was telling him the intricacies of grinding feed, he was gesturing the moves with his left hand, and arm. They seemed, to have a mind of their own, working only when he wasn't aware, the rest of the time, laying motionless on the bed.

Our room had a couch, that made into a bed. All of the rooms were private, so at night I had a place to sleep. He was very restless, and upset tonight, so I laid on the bed with him. We wanted so bad to hold, and comfort each other. I was on his left side, and with him not able to put his left arm around me, it was an exercise in futility. Or so I thought. I reached, and struggled to grasp behind me, and finally grabbed his left arm, pulled it around me. Desperately tried, to find some comfort, in my husband's arms. I laid there, till he fell asleep, then I crawled over to my makeshift bed, and tried to get some sleep.

I was awakened every time, he needed to go to the bathroom, which was quite often. I helped the aides walk him to the bathroom, and I sat with him. Someone had to remain with him, he couldn't remember, he was not supposed to get up by himself. So I sat with him, and we talked. He was disturbed by the fact, his arm, and leg, were not cooperating with him. One night, as we sat in the bathroom, he said to me, "We have to name this dud," meaning his arm. "It doesn't work, what can we name it?" Having always had a quirky sense of humor, I offered up the most logical names, like "Ed" or "Bob," after those erectile dysfunction commercials. I thought, it made sense to me. Phill, however, did not agree. He didn't seem to think, they were funny. When our aide came back, to help us back to bed, he asked her opinion. She offered up, "Mayhem," after the Allstate commercial. That too, seemed most appropriate. Mayhem was born.

Day 5

We seemed to be establishing a routine. We would get up, I helped Phill get washed up, and in a chair, ready for the kids to come in, or other visitors to stop by. The doctor stopped by, and told us, about a great stroke Rehab Facility nearby. He recommended Phill, be admitted there, for therapy. He would need extensive therapy, if he hoped to regain the use of his left arm, and leg. Phill said, he was willing to go. I was, somewhat apprehensive. I had been staying around the clock, with him since his stroke, and at the Rehab Facility, I would have to go home. I was unsure, how he would do alone. I didn't voice my concerns to anyone. I didn't want to worry him, over the move.

I took some time to run home for the first time since we were admitted. The kids had all been looking for Phill's teeth. No one, had been able to find them. After thirty-one years with this man, I was fairly certain, I knew how his mind worked, and would be able back track, until I found them. Although, the uneasy thought, had crept into my head, was he confused downstairs? Could he, have wrapped them in a napkin, as he had done, numerous times, and thrown them in the fire, with the napkin? That was a distinct possibility. I hoped not! I knew he had taken my jeans, off the line downstairs, and brought them upstairs for me. (We have a clothesline downstairs near the woodstove, to dry clothes, We use it, instead of always using the dryer. I hated my jeans dried, in the dryer.) So, I began my search near the clothes line. It didn't take long to find, what I was looking for. Laying on the couch, under the clothes line, was the object of my search. He had placed the teeth, wrapped in a napkin, there, while he took down my jeans. I was relieved! I headed back to the hospital, my mission was complete.

Chapter 4

Day 6

Today marked the beginning of a new chapter. Rehab. They found a bed at the stroke facility. Phill was transported by ambulance to the new facility. He seemed okay with whatever was going on. He was still showing that child-like happiness at times. I was not sure if he realized, or not, that I wouldn't be able to stay with him. Even though I had told him, he was still unable to retain conversations for any length of time. The ambulance loaded him up, and left. I stopped downstairs to say goodbye to our friend, Audrey, and some of the girls she worked with, that I had come to know quite well. One of the girls, took a hold of my hands, and looked me hard in the eyes, "You are going to have to be strong!" She said. "In a few days he is going to beg you, to bring him home. You are going to have to be strong, and tell him no!" She finished with "This will be his only way of overcoming this, and you will have to say NO!" I was crying. There was too much pent up emotion. I felt like, I needed to just get through this.

I arrived at Rehab, and found Phill in a ward with two other men. His bed was by the window. He was upset, and stressed. When he first arrived, he was taken to the bathroom, and sat on a potty chair, that the other men had used. Phill has always had issues, using public bathrooms. The stroke magnified those issues. He told me, he was cold. In the hospital, they automatically started him on a blood thinner for the A-fib, called Xeralto. It made him feel the cold more. The windows were old, and he could feel a draft. The other hospital, was a brand new hospital, the rehab center, was an old building. To him, it felt dirty, and shoddy. No amount of reassurance, would convince him, otherwise.

All of the different therapists, who would be working with him, came in to meet, and assess his condition. He was happily distracted by the activity going on around him. Two of the PT staff, arrived with a walker, and a waist belt, to walk him. I took a video, of them trying to walk him with a walker. His left hand could not grasp, nor hang on to the walker. He was not even aware, he had a left hand. After a few minutes, they gave up on the walker. The two of them, staggered through the door, with Phill in the middle, into the hallway. It was not pretty. Phill's left foot, and leg had no idea, where they were supposed to be. As the three of them started down the hall, the head of PT, came out to check out Phill's progress. I watched them stagger from one side of the hall, to the other for a few minutes, I then asked PT, if I could show them, what we had been doing in the hospital. The head therapist was interested. I took Phill's hands in mine, and I asked one of the PT staff, to put her hands on his waist from behind. I told Phill, "Look only at me, stand up tall," and we began to walk. The therapist was impressed with, what we had accomplished with, just simple eye contact. He decided the aides, should use that method of walking him, in his room. I felt like they had his best interests at heart. I could go home with some measure of peace.

Jenny was coming in to help him with supper so that I could go home, and get some rest. My hands felt like they were made of lead as they rested on the steering wheel. I drove the sixty miles home in a daze. I kissed my mom, and headed for my bed. The phone rang. It was Jenny, she said Phill wanted to tell me goodnight. Our conversation was very short. He was ready to get off the phone, after only a few minutes. This was so different, than the pre-stroke Phill, who, when I traveled, would want to stay on the phone for an hour. Sometimes, while he read a farm magazine, or watched TV, he just didn't want to hang up with me. Jenny returned to the phone, and told me, he refused his dinner. He wouldn't eat any of it, and she was unsure why. I told her not to worry about it, I would talk to him in the morning. I was just too weary to worry about it. Jenny has always been very close to her dad. She, being the oldest girl has always held the most special place in her daddy's heart. As a little girl, Jenny did everything with gusto, whether it was driving a three wheeler, motorcycle, or racing the other kids, she had to be the fastest, or the biggest daredevil. More than once, we had to take a break, from motorized vehicles, in an effort to keep her safe. She was her daddy's daughter, and the fruit didn't fall far from the tree. This stroke hit her hard. It hit us all hard.

Day 7

I arrived at Rehab to find Phill extremely anxious, and upset. He said, he froze all night. They pulled the blinds, but it didn't help. The gentleman in the bed opposite, was coughing so bad, Phill was now convinced, the man had pneumonia, and he would catch it. The man developed some breathing issues in the night, between the nurses working with him, and all the commotion, Phill had been upset terribly. He thought the man was dying. He became convinced, he would die in here, too. Finally, towards morning, one of the aides moved him to the open bed, away from the window. He was crying, and so upset. He became adamant, he was not staying here. I now understood, why Phill refused to eat his dinner last night. He was stressed, and inconsolable. Nothing, I said, reassured him. I called Young Phill, and told him what was happening, he told me, he would be here soon, to help figure this out. In the meantime, he called his siblings to update them.

Tamy, our daughter from Buffalo, had gone to Wyoming, to visit Jamie. A trip that had been planned, months before the stroke. Her dad, insisted she go. My phone rang, it was Tamy and Jamie, I headed for the ladies room, so Phill wouldn't hear our conversation. They told me, I had to make him stay. I tried to explain, that I was trying my best. But, at the end of the day, he, was an adult, who had the legal right, to sign himself out, against my wishes. I became so overwhelmed, and frustrated, that I hung up. As I headed back to the room, I reminded myself, "I was doing, the best I could do." The girls called back. Jamie asked to speak to her dad. A few minutes later, he threw the phone on the bed, and wouldn't even look at it. He did not want to hear what Jamie had to say. He could not believe that she would talk to him that way. I picked up the phone, and told her he was all done talking. At which point Tamy said, "Mom, could I talk to him?" I told her, "You can try." It wasn't only a few minutes, and the phone again, flew on the bed. He looked away, wouldn't even look at it. I picked it up again, and said, "He's all done talking." Both girls were crying. Being nurses, they both knew the ramifications if their dad did not complete this program. Their attempts to chastise him into staying, were met with a stony silence. He was not interested in hearing their reasons, why he should stay.

The doctor, and one of the nurses were the next ones through the door. Phill told the doctor about the draft, and that he had a sore throat. The doctor was not interested, nor responsible for the architecture of the building, we were informed. I was shocked. How could someone talk to him this way? This was a complete contrast to what, we had experienced so far, from the rest of the staff, and therapists. I asked if we could move him to another room, the immediate response was, "No." The doctor looked at his throat, and said he had thrush. A common complaint in stroke patients.

After they left, Phill said, "I don't think they even listened to me." I told him that I didn't think they listened either. He looked so scared, and vulnerable that my heart ached for him. All that he wanted was to come home. He didn't feel safe. All I wanted, was to bring him home! He was crying, and pleaded with me, "Please won't you take me home? Please? My kids would help you take care of me, please?" It was like someone had plunged a knife into my chest and was turning the blade slowly, causing such immense pain, that I could not breathe. I was sobbing. My husband, always so fiercely independent, my rock, my love, was sobbing begging me to bring him home. There are no words to describe how devastating this was to me. I was lost.

15

Soon, Young Phill and Jenny arrived. Jenny put an arm around me, and said, "Come on we are going for coffee." Young Phill would stay with his dad. I let her lead me away. Over coffee, I told Jenny what had transpired that morning. While we were talking, I decided to look up some information on Phill's stroke. I found that large rooms, like the ward he was currently in, could cause extreme anxiety in stroke patients.

While we were gone Young Phill had a long conversation with his dad. He told him, that he needed to stay, if he ever wanted to go back to farming. Young Phill gently informed him that none of us have the education, or the know how to help him, and all worked full time jobs. He also said, that it wasn't fair to me, for Phill to try to make me bring him home, when he needed to stay. Phill agreed to stay a couple of days. With Phill's inability to gauge time, we were hopeful that we bought some time.

When Jenny and I got back to the room, they were taking Phill to PT. Jenny went with him to PT. Young Phill and I talked to Kelly, who was from another farm family in our area. She was a Case Manager. We asked again for them to change his room. Kelly told me they have more patients coming in, and needed the empty rooms. I explained that they would still have the same amount of rooms. He just needed his room exchanged, for one that was smaller. I explained what I had found in my search about large rooms, and stroke patients. Kelly told us she couldn't promise anything, but she would see what she could do. We went back to watch Phill work in PT.

Kelly returned, and told us that they had moved Phill to a smaller room. After his therapies, we headed to his new room. He promptly laid down, and fell asleep. I was relieved. While Phill was resting, the kids, and I went for coffee. They proceeded to tell me; they have decided that I was not staying, with their dad at night, till he goes to bed. I had to leave at four, or five p.m. One of them, would come be with him, through his dinner, and help him get ready for bed. I was so very proud of them. It felt very funny, to walk out, and leave them, but I was washed out, from all of the emotions. I drove home. I spent a few minutes with Mom, then headed for our room. I turned on the TV, and just laid there. I didn't want to talk to anyone. I just wanted to be alone, sort through all of the events from today. I wondered, how will we ever be able to get through this? My prayer tonight was for strength.

Chapter 5

Day 8

I tried to leave the house early every morning so that I could be at Rehab by 7:30 a.m. to make sure Phill had eaten something before his therapy sessions. Phill's therapy included Speech Therapy, Occupational Therapy, and Physical Therapy geared to help combat his deficits. Speech used several kinds of tools to improve not just his speech, but the muscle control on his affected side also. Of all the therapies, he hates Speech, the most. Phill said, he felt embarrassed to do funny faces, and exercises in front of two young beautiful women. His first session, he had a terrible time concentrating on the tasks at hand. Because of the stroke, the filter that tells him what is, or, is not, appropriate to say, had been damaged, if he thought it, he spoke it. He would tell his therapist Kim *(not her real name), "Did anyone ever tell you that you have the cutest little button nose?" I have to admit, it made me chuckle. The girls worked very hard, to keep him on task. This was hard to see, because, had they known him before the stroke, they would know he had always been very task driven. They worked on getting his muscles in, and around his mouth to work. They also did some written tasks, where he had to figure out the answers to the questions by eliminating other answers. Phill hated those "tests", as he called them, with a passion. They reminded him of the achievement tests you have to take in school. He did not excel in school, and those tests always made him feel stupid. These assignments brought back those feelings, and no amount of reassurance, that it was not a pass/fail situation; it was only a tool to retrain his brain, helped. He was totally frustrated, and upset every time they brought those out. After every session he felt like he had failed. It was hard to see him so distraught, and not be able to help him understand, that it isn't what he thought.

Occupational Therapy would help rewire Phill's brain. I was amazed at the simplest of tasks that brought this process about. They taught him to dress himself, use his left arm, and hand for everyday tasks. They worked towards his brain recognizing his left side. It was amazing to watch!

I began to notice a pattern with Phill's therapy. When he was uncomfortable with what was going on in therapy, he became short of breath. He would say he couldn't breathe. I had brought in some Vicks Vapor rub to help with his stuffiness, from the dry air in the Rehab. I got him to try a little under his nose, and the mentholated smell seemed to calm him. It opened up his sinuses, and he could breathe. He began to carry the jar in his pocket, and when he felt stressed it soothed him. I felt I was, becoming a master at problem solving. When faced with the obstacles that we had been presented with, sometimes you have to think outside the box. For example, Phill had Carpal Tunnel Syndrome in both wrists for years which had caused numbness in both hands. Holding on to a Styrofoam cup to drink after the stroke was a huge challenge. Instead, I asked one of the nurses for another cup that he could hang on to, and she found a drinking cup for children that had two handles. He could use either one or, both hands, and be able to control it. Problem solved! I knew him better than anyone else in the world, I needed to look for solutions in things that gave him comfort, and were familiar to him.

Day 9

Today they got in a good workout, and he was very tired. Phill had to propel himself down the hall, and around the corner to PT, with his legs. He had to put his heel down first just like he was walking. The left leg was really clumsy, but he tried. It was hard work. He had to also keep track of his left arm, and hand to be sure it didn't end up in the spokes of the wheelchair. He still "loses it" quite regularly. One evening while Jenny was there for his dinner, his left hand came up, and planted itself in the middle of his dinner plate. He was unaware of where his hand was until, Jenny asked him if he knew where it was. Then he started looking for it, and found it nestled in the middle of his plate. They both laughed at the absurdity of having to find your hand. When you stop, and think about it, I can only imagine how disconcerting it would be to have to one day search for your hand because you have no idea of its location. The body's ability to totally neglect something, as fundamental as an arm, hand, or leg was mind boggling. Phill told me, how he laid in bed one night, and put his right hand on the top of his head where he encountered another hand which he did not recognize. It was his left hand, and it scared him to death. He didn't know whose hand he had found, and because of the neglect, he couldn't feel his left hand on his head. We talked about how his left hand could recognize his right hand, but his right hand couldn't recognize his left. How strange that must have been for him. I told Phill he was lucky he didn't encounter his left hand under the covers, and not realize whose hand it was. That would be scary! Phill didn't think I was funny. I, on the other hand, found myself, totally amusing, and had a good long laugh!

I want to take a minute to talk about Phill's Physical Therapist Brian. What an amazing person. He was so compassionate, and understanding of what Phill was going through, yet able to keep him on task, and motivated, just by the way he talked, and listened to him. Phill responded well to Brian. I could see progress in his walking just in the few days. I was so glad, that we were able, to convince him to stay. I shuddered to think, of what the outcome would have been, had he refused to stay.

I learned so much myself, about what it took, to retrain the brain. I was a little sponge, absorbing as much as I could. This was so outside the realm of anything we, as his family could have accomplished, at home, without this assistance. I tried to video his progress every day, and post it on the Facebook Page Jenny had set up. Family, and friends could keep up with Phill's progress without me being tied to a phone all day. Family members started posting videos of themselves on the page for Phill, They wished him good luck, letting him know they loved him, and were praying for him. These posts made him laugh, and cry at the same time. Some, so funny they brightened his day. Our granddaughter Laura, who is in the Navy, has been stationed half a world away, in Japan. She sent her Papa a video telling him she loved him, and missed him, blowing him kisses across the miles. We both cried. I missed her so much.

Day 10

Every day as I headed into Rehab, I found myself trying to anticipate the mood I would find Phill in. More mornings than not, he was stressed when I arrived, and wouldn't even look at me. This too, a side effect of the stroke. Even the simplest things would throw him into a tailspin, and he is unable to cope. I found on these mornings, I needed to be super positive. To reassure him that everything would be okay, that I was here, and I would make sure nothing happened to him. I was his protector. I redirected the conversation about therapy, or anything happening outside Rehab. Today I came armed with a new weapon! Homemade Cream of Broccoli Soup! It is one of his favorites. I brought a crock pot full for him, and the staff at Rehab. I knew he would enjoy the soup better than hospital food, and I wanted to thank the staff for the excellent care they had given Phill. He was so excited for his lunch today!

Just before the therapist came to get Phill, my phone rang, and it was Young Phill. He called to let me know how things were going on the farm. He had to pick up the reins, and between him, and Merlin, who came the day of the stroke, they have taken care of everything on the farm. Because of that, I could be at the hospital, and not worried about things at home. It was just as stressful for Young Phill, taking on the extra work, and trying to do it the way he knew his dad would want it done. His son, Ben, picked up the slack at Young Phill's coal business, so he was able to take over for us. I think that was kind of the way it should be, family helping family. After we discussed how things were going, Young Phill just started to cry on the phone. It broke my heart. I knew we were both scared of the same thing, yet neither of us wanted to voice it. What if. What if his dad could never farm again? What if he didn't get better? He would be devastated beyond measure. Young Phill said he was sorry for crying, but, he to let it go. I told him, "I know." Only it seemed I was unable, to really let go.

In PT, Brian had Phill walking with a hemi walker. It kind of resembled a folded up ladder, with a rounded top, and four legs. Phill could hold it with just his right hand, and move it to walk. Brian used a belt around Phill's waist for safety, but he was motoring kind of on his own. It was great to see.

I would like to talk about the people who took care of Phill on a daily basis, his care partners. They were responsible for taking care of his daily needs, such as bathing, changing his bed, bathroom duties, and bringing his food tray. Just being there for his everyday needs. They were all so kind, and caring, but a few, really stood apart from everyone else. Paulette, is one who went above, and beyond. She made Phill as comfortable as possible, under the circumstances, that he had been put in. He hated having someone wipe his butt, or bathe him. He, naturally, was embarrassed beyond belief. Paulette engaged him in conversation, and kept him distracted with jokes. Her bubbly personality shined through, as she took time to listen to him, and helped him to understand everything, that happened to him. On one of the bath days, Phill was distraught. The day before, when I was taking him to the bathroom, he was upset about all that had happened to him, and the way things were going. I tried to explain, that a lot of what he was feeling, was from the stroke. He didn't like that answer, and was upset. He told me, he was tired of "pat answers". He was angry, and seemed, I thought, rude. I, told him, that he did not get to be disrespectful to me. Lesson one for me. I was not dealing with the same man, that I had for over thirty years. The pre-stroke Phill would have just told me he wasn't being disrespectful, and let it go. After the stroke, he was unable to deal with those emotions. Everything seemed magnified. He was up all night fretting, and emotional, afraid that I thought, he was disrespecting me, and he would never do that. During his shower the next morning, he was very upset. He told Paulette, how he feared, I thought he had been disrespectful to me. She patiently helped him calm down, and explained, she was sure that I knew he didn't mean to sound disrespectful, and was just upset at the circumstances. By the time I arrived, he had calmed considerably. He could get emotional even now, talking about this.

Another Care Partner that should be recognized for her kindness is Angel. Her name described, who she really was. Phill had been in the bathroom, put his light on, to signal he was finished. Angel, was the one, who answered his call light. This was one of Phill's bad days. He had been extremely emotional, and must have looked so lost. I have seen that look, it had been our constant companion since the stroke. When Angel opened up the bathroom door to help Phill, she must have seen his distress, and felt his pain. She reached over, and gave him a hug. A simple little squeeze, a seemingly small gesture that touched not just my husband's heart, but mine as well. That was the true meaning of kindness.

Chapter 6

Day 11

Sunday arrived, and Phill was having a ball. He had quite a few visitors. Our next door neighbor, Frank came all the way down to see us. Frank moved in down the road when Phill was nine years old. They have been lifelong neighbors, and friends. A couple of years ago, Frank, and his wife, Karen's home caught fire. Phill, along with, another neighbor went into the burning house to get Karen out. Both men were nominated for the Carnegie Medal of Honor, and given plaques from the fire department for their bravery. Phill hated all the attention, felt he hadn't done anything, that anyone else wouldn't have done. He was a hero to both Frank, and Karen. So Frank drove sixty miles to come, and check up on him. Carl, another neighbor, who used to be our Cooperative Extension Agent for years, brought another neighbor down to visit Phill. They all laughed, and joked. Phill and Carl were always trading barbs with each other. It was great to see Phill laughing, enjoying their company. Gary, is a fellow farmer from our neck of the woods. He and Phill go way back. A few years ago, Gary was severely injured when his tractor seat broke, dumping him off the back of the tractor in between the tractor, and manure spreader. The tractor rolled backwards over top of Gary, injuring him severely. He was laid up for months. Phill called Gary a lot throughout his convalescence. Gary, made the trip to visit us, and repay the favor. A close friend, Huck made the trip. We met years ago, when we both purchased cows at an auction, that had been contaminated by Bovine Tuberculosis. It was a stressful time. We, however, managed to become fast friends, and have remained close for years. At times like these, you find out how much people really care about you. We are humbled. It was a wonderful day! I headed home when Young Phill arrived.

Day 12

Monday brought us back into the swing of things. Pt was interesting. Brian gave Phill a stick, and had him hold on each end with both hands. Brian, then threw a beach ball, and Phill had to hit it with the stick. This helped him to raise both arms to the same level at the same time. Phill did pretty good! Next, Phill stood in the hall with his walker. Another therapist, was holding small orange cones, that he had to reach for with his left hand, and then his right. This worked on increasing his balance as well as his ability to grasp, and hold on to things with his left hand. Phill had worked with the cones before, when sitting down, and reaching, but this was the first time he had been standing, and reaching.

I went to talk to Kim and Alicia, Phill's speech therapists. He had been stressed every time he worked on the word games. They explained, one of the things they were working on was keeping him on task. They told me, he had struggled tremendously with this. I asked if it were okay if I brought in a milker for him to assemble, and disassemble. They would see how well he could stay on task, and agreed it was a good idea. It felt really good to be able to help, if only a little. I hated the fact, they only knew this man, not the one he used to be. I found that really bothered me. I understood in my head that they had to work with, what they were presented with. My heart only wanted them to know the man he used to be, before this stroke devastated our lives, and made him someone who couldn't stay on task, or remember one day, from the next. It was just hard.

Jenny came in today, and relieved me. I decided to meet a friend of mine, Audrey, for dinner. I hadn't had time to see anyone since Phill's stroke. It was a good distraction.

Chapter 7

Day 13

Today marked one week in Rehab. In the beginning, I was unsure we would even see a few days, let alone a full week. Today was Phill's first evaluation. This was a meeting, with all of his therapists, doctors, and caregivers, each giving their perspective on his progression. We were not allowed to go to this meeting. After the meeting Kelly, our case manager, told us that we would be here, at least another week. They would reconvene the following week for a new assessment. Phill took the news better than I thought he would. He was still afraid at night, and convinced he was going to die there, all alone. Nothing I said seemed to change that thought. I was sad, that he felt so alone. It broke my heart. In the long run, his need for this therapy was far more important than his fear. If he was to return to farming, we needed to stay.

Today also marked a moving day. Walter*(not his real name), Phill's roommate, was released to go home. We were sad to see him go. Walter was confused most of the time, and always tried to get out of bed unassisted, setting off all kinds of alarms. He always had something funny to say, even when he told me, I "ratted" him out to the nurses, when he tried to escape. We missed his antics. Tonight was Phill's first night alone in his room. I was apprehensive about how it would go. Jenny was there tonight, and brought him a Five Guys Burger for his dinner. Later he told me he liked the burger when he called to say goodnight. He sounded upbeat, and happy. I thought it might go okay.

Day 14

Today I brought in my mom's famous Key Lime Cake. Phill had always loved this cake. I was certain the nurses, and caregivers would too. It was another Thank You, for their kindness, and care.

When I came in Phill, was already working with Zoe, an OT Therapist. They were working on dressing. I could see he was struggling. He had a problem holding onto his pants, or shorts with his left hand, then being able to pick up his left foot, and put it into the pants leg. He was frustrated. When he saw me, he said, "Hey hon, could you help me?" Zoe, and I both said "NO!" We both giggled. She explained to him, he had to learn to do this by himself. Phill kept working until, he finally got his underwear, and shorts on. This was a major accomplishment. One, he would have to keep working on. I brought in tee shirts for Phill to wear, but he claimed they were too warm. He would rather wear the short sleeved button up shirts, instead. Tina, and Zoe taught him to button the shirt part way, then put it over his head like a tee shirt, after which he could continue buttoning it up. With the loss of feeling in both hands, from carpal tunnel surgery, combined, with the loss of feeling on the left side from the stroke, this became a monumental project, which caused more than a few angry words. They were sure that he would eventually, be able to accomplish this. Tina worked with Phill during the week, and Zoe filled in on the weekends. Tina had such an understanding of what Phill was going through. She helped him manage his feelings, and some of the simple tasks he had to relearn. One day, when I was a little overwhelmed, with everything we had been through, she took a minute, to rub my shoulder, and let me know, I wasn't alone. Such a tiny little gesture, really, but so very meaningful to me. Those little things that we sometimes pass off as not really important, to someone else, may feel like a life ring in the middle of the ocean. Zoe, was just so darn cute. She was bubbly, and had the greatest smile. She had so much patience. When she worked with Phill, she would wait for him to figure things out, guiding him

27

just by her presence. She made him feel less self conscious, while she taught him to dress himself.

We started week two, therapies were starting to ramp up. In PT, Phill walked with the hemi walker some of the way down to the PT area. He did real well. Once there, Phill worked on balance, and standing while doing another task. Today, he was putting color coded rings on a peg with his left hand. Brian was giving him directions as to which color, Phill had to figure out which peg that color went on. This was so interesting to watch. Brian had a variety of tasks that challenged Phill, each, more difficult than the previous. All in all, Phill did pretty good. It was amazing to watch the improvements.

In Speech today, Alicia and Kim had Phill assemble, and disassemble the milker that I had brought in. He did fairly good at staying on task. Not once did he need the Vicks. I could see that he had some real anxiety issues, especially pertaining to problem solving on paper. He still struggled immensely with those.

OT had Phill, taking color coded clothespins, and putting them on the corresponding color on a piece of cardboard. Some of the colors were only slightly different shades of the same color. He really had to study the color. Pinching the clothespin worked his fine motor skills. Phill was really intrigued with this game, and asked if he could take it back to his room. Tina let him, as long as he promised to work on it. We played with it several times throughout the day. She had also given Phill this little brush, that he was to use on his left side. He had to brush from joint to joint in the same direction. This helped with the hypersensitivity on his left side. Phill liked how it felt, when he used it.

The improvements that had come about just in one week were truly astonishing. In the beginning Phill couldn't move his left arm or hand on command. After one week, he was able to use his left arm to place rings on pegs. Pinch little clothespins, and place them on a piece of cardboard. It was unbelievable how fast the brain compensated.

Rick* (not his real name), our new roommate, moved in. He was older than Phill, but, very sharp. He had been sent to Rehab after an illness. Phill wanted to keep the drape between them closed. So closed it stayed…for now.

Therapy always made Phill exhausted. I, too felt the strain, so I laid down with him, and we napped.

Chapter 8

Day 15

I heard Phill's voice before I even reached the room. He was laughing! I was amazed to hear him laugh like that. Not since the stroke, had he sounded like this. It was wonderful to hear. I turned the corner into the room, and was amazed to see the curtain between the two beds, open. Both men were just chatting away. It made me smile. Phill greeted me with, "Hi Beautiful!" I said, "Hi Yourself." I could see that these two have forged a bond. I was glad. Normally, Phill loved to talk. Since his stroke however, he had been limited to mostly me, and the therapists. They, however, spend a great deal of time redirecting him, not to talk as much during sessions. He now had a friend.

Today Phill would be shaving himself. He looked rather scruffy. Phill's face had been so hypersensitive, the razor on his face had been more input, than he could bear. I pushed him up to the sink, adjusted the mirror, so he could see himself. He lathered the shaving crème, while I, reminded him to shave the left side of his face. He did a great job on the right side. He struggled with under his chin, as well as, the left side of his face. With some coaxing he did a fair job with those areas. I was pleased. I gave him a kiss, and told him how much I loved him. He worked so hard. I was proud of him.

I found out what a character Rick was, when the med nurse came in. She always asked, "What's your name?" Rick replied, "Rick Tunner," then spelled, "S. M. I. T. H." I started laughing, and so did she. Yes, he was a corker.

Day 16

I was not feeling so well. I had been diagnosed with Reactive Airway Disease, and was feeling the effects of carrying tires in the car. I had taken our car in to exchange the winter tires, for summer ones. I did not want to take time to unload them, before I left for the hospital yesterday. It was quite warm where I parked the car, and the sun heated up the tires inside the car. When I left to go home the smell was very strong, and I had a reaction to it. I hadn't wanted to take time, to go to the doctor, I wanted to just be with Phill. I was, however, coughing quite a bit, and felt terrible.

A wonderful thing happened, Phill, with the help of daughter, Tamy, bought me a beautiful card. Phill was so happy when he gave it to me. It made me cry. Today, I remembered how blessed I really was. I thanked God for these little blessings.

Today, in PT, Phill had to navigate through, and around these orange cones when he walked. He was still having problems on the left, but did a fair job. The progress he has made was amazing to watch.

These days seemed surreal. I looked out the window, the sun was shining. People were going about their lives, except for us. We were just trying to get through this. Find a way to deal with all that had happened. There was a sense of loss. I don't know if I can explain it, but our lives seemed to belong to someone else. This wasn't our life! Phill had always been so strong, so vital. Never, could I have imagined him, being so lost, so vulnerable. He has bulled through all of the surgeries, he has had in the last few years, to get better. A few years back, the doctor told us Phill had a five centimeter tumor on his left kidney. When I asked if it was malignant, the doctor told me ninety-eight percent of them are. We were told, Phill had spots on his liver, and spleen. It looked very much like he had cancer, and there was a good chance it may have spread. Even then, he was determined. We would get through what ever happened. He was right of course, it turned out that he was in the two percent, the tumor was benign. The spots turned out to be hemangiomas, which are what make up birth marks. Phill was cleared. Seeing him so determined before, made seeing him, unable to take care of the most basic, of needs, so tough. It was hard to believe that God would save him from cancer, give him such a miracle, only to strike him down with a stroke. It seemed so impossible, but I knew that God had a plan. We just didn't know what it was. I still had my faith, and right now it had to be my rock. It was all I had.

Day 17

I was excited, today. Tamy, our son in law, Steve, and their three children came all the way from Buffalo, to see us. I knew the kids were really excited, to see Phill. The last time they saw him, was the morning of the stroke, and they watched him being taken away in the ambulance. I so worried, how all that happened, would affect them. I had to laugh, when Tamy, told me about her conversation with the kids after Phill's stroke. Tamy asked the kids, if they understood what had happened to Big Pa? Aiden, the youngest, gave his rendition of the events of that morning. "Big Pa had a little stroke, and Nana said, sit down. Big Pa wouldn't listen, so Nana said, YOU SIT DOWN!" I said to Tamy, "Oh great, I traumatized them." Tamy said, "No, Aiden just thought Big Pa should have listened to Nana!" Kids have such a wonderful way of looking at things! They don't have to analyze everything. It's all kind of taken, at face value.

When the kids came today, Zoe brought her Big Pa a piece of paper she had decorated it, telling him how he is such a wonderful grandpa. Phill was so touched. He has always been a worker. Farming is a twenty-four/seven commitment, which meant he spent a lot of time working when the kids were visiting. He felt, he hadn't been around as much as he should have. Zoe, however, didn't feel that way, and let him know with a simple piece of paper. Zane, and Aiden, were more interested in riding in Phill's wheelchair, so we let them motor around the room.

While Phill took a nap, Tamy, her family, and I, went in the room next door, that served as a lunchroom. There were chairs, and tables along with some games. We played several hands of hearts, and visited about Phill's progress. It was a great day!

A very interesting thing happened this morning in OT. Zoe, (the therapist), used a vibrator, that looked like a large belt sander, on Phill's left leg. He immediately startled, and twitched. He told Zoe, that it sent an electrical shock up his body, and into his brain. Zoe told us, we should write these things down, because, usually people with Phill's degree of stroke cannot communicate these things, and maybe it could help someone else.

Day 18

Today brought us another round of visitors. I helped Phill shower, and got him ready, for today's round of company. I sat, and read while he napped. He was still very emotional, and cried often. I do have to say, that since Rick has become his roommate, he has been in better spirits when I come in. It was good to see.

The afternoon brought our neighbor, Frank, again, to check on Phill's progress. Our granddaughter Amanda, her fiancée, and great granddaughter, Aubrey, all came to see papa. That is what our older grandchildren, have always called Phill. The younger grandchildren, call him, "Big Pa". Tamy, and Steve's children, call Steve, "Papa", creating the need for a different name to call Phill. Some of the other neighbors, from the hill also made the trek down to visit with us. It was a long, busy day for Phill. He was tired, so was I.

Chapter 9

Day 19

In PT, Brian had Phill work on turns. He turned, both, to the left, and right, as well, as side step. He was supposed to stop before he reached the wall. Phill bumped in to the wall, on the left, but after a few tries, it registered that the wall was there.

In speech, Alicia and Kim used a small vibrating apparatus to stimulate the muscles in Phill's face. With everything on the left side so hypersensitive, the input was uncomfortable. They also had him try to smile, while they applied pressure to the cheek muscles, to strengthen them. I could see progress when he tried to put his teeth in. The first week, he had a tremendous amount of trouble actually getting them in his mouth correctly. He would put them in, then I would look, and the teeth would be sideways in his mouth, he wouldn't realize it. So, I would slip them into place. Now the lips on the left side move, and don't get caught up on the dentures.

Tina put Phill in a large bag, that was made to restrain. It stimulated input, by putting equal pressure on both sides. His arms were at his sides, and he was to push against the bag. He was not fond of being restrained. Our pickup had rolled on top of him once, while he was working on it. The truck pinned him. He, ended up with a broken arm, and bruises. The end of a hammer handle, he was using, had poked him in the stomach, and left a perfect round imprint, in the form, of a bruise. Phill wasn't really comfortable, with this whole procedure. It wasn't tight enough to really confine him, and he was able to work through it.

We headed back to our room, Phill was really tired, and truthfully so was I. Between being sick, and all, that had transpired, last two weeks of my life, had been grueling. Soon, I headed home. Son, Brian came in, and relieved me. I knew Phill would have a good evening with Brian, he always enjoyed talking with his youngest son. Brian was the child most like his father in so many ways. Brian, once gave us a picture of himself dressed up for Halloween. He was supposed to be his dad. He looked just like him! It was really uncanny, just how much they looked alike. The two of them had a solid connection with each other, in a special way. That bond was even stronger now.

I finally broke down, and went to the doctor today. It was, as I suspected, a reaction, to the odor of the tires. It caused a form of bronchitis. Armed with antibiotics, and steroids, I headed back to the hospital. Phill was relieved that I went.

Day 20

The second evaluation day was today. Everyone who worked with him, along with the doctors, and social workers met, and decided whether, or not his progress was enough for Phill to go home. I knew he had made great strides, but was it enough for Rehab, to feel comfortable sending him home? Was he where they wanted him to be, at this stage? These were the questions that ran through my mind. Time would tell whether or not his progress was enough.

In PT, Brian walked Phill without his walker today. Brian gave him a rod to hang on to, and put a waist belt on him. He walked him down the hall. I shook with emotion, as I watched Phill motor on his own! Time seemed suspended, as he first placed his right foot forward, then his left moved forward. Brian had him, check the position of the left foot, so it would be ready, for the next step. I found I was actually holding my breath, in anticipation of the next step. Each time he moved that leg in the right direction, I let my breath out. It was apparent, that as long as his concentration, and focus stayed on track, he walked great! If his concentration wandered so did he. I noticed the first time we walked Phill after the stroke, that concentration, and focus were a huge part in keeping him upright. If you added anything to the equation, it threw him off, and he would have problems. Even something as simple, as having his dentures in when he walked, would break his focus. Phill has never been one, to wear his dentures all the time, so they weren't something, his body was used to. When they walked him, and he had his dentures in, they felt foreign to him, and concentration was broken. Once early on, while we were still in the hospital, we came out of the bathroom, there was a mirror on the wall, facing us. Phill saw himself for the first time since the stroke. He lost his concentration, and almost fell over. He said, it looked like his dad, standing there. Just, simple little things, can be such a game changer. It is all about the input. How the brain processes elements in his surroundings.

Kelly came after the meeting, to let us know that the team felt, Phill could be released towards the end of the week. Oh, happy day! I looked forward to having Phill home, and life resuming its normal course. Looking back, I don't think that I realized all, that this meant. Life's normal course had been altered, the day Phill had the stroke. I really did not have any idea, of what life, was going to be like, when we returned home. I was just happy to be able to finally take my husband home.

Chapter 10

Day 21

When I arrived this morning, Phill was already dressed, and ready to start the day. After I took care of his clean clothes, he said, he wanted to talk to me. I sat down on the bed, and he told me that he wanted to renew our wedding vows. I didn't quite know what to say. Years ago, I had asked Phill to renew our vows. He was adamant, that he didn't want to. His argument was; that he had already married one woman twice, and he wasn't going to do it again. I told him, the trick was not to get divorced in between! Phill had been married a couple of times before me, and he had married, and divorced this lady twice. I didn't say anything about, how he felt previously felt about this subject, I just said okay. In my mind however, I decided that stroke, or no stroke, he would have to take care of this on his own, I felt that if it was, so important to him, he would find a way. Maybe that sounded a little harsh, but I did not want to feel that I had taken advantage of this situation. Phill wanted Steve, our son in law, to do the service, He wanted only our kids, and grandkids, and my mother there. I did make one request, for our youngest daughter Jamie's, best friend Danielle, and her husband Pasha, to be there. Danielle, is like one of our kids. Phill agreed. It would be up to him to put his plan in action. We would see.

With a release date now official, we still had a few days, to get as much of the remaining therapy, as we could. In PT, Brian had upgraded Phill to a special cane with four legs, and retired the hemi walker. Walking down the hall, with the new cane, was a new experience, for him. It handled differently, and was not quite as steady, as the hemi was. Even with four legs, the cane had some movement, which required more balance. Brian believed he, was ready for progression, to the cane. The maiden voyage, didn't go half bad. Phill had a few balance issues, but he was able to compensate, and all in all, it went well. He would go home with the cane. That made him happy.

Phill's left arm came up while he was walking. It either, went out to the side, or up, like he was using it for balance. Brian reminded him to try to keep it down. He put it in his pocket. That seemed to help.

Part of Phill's OT therapy, as I have said before, was learning to dress himself. He has been doing fairly well at this task. However, he became very agitated, when he couldn't find, the arm hole. Or get his pants on, and up, buttoned, and zipped. His belt gave him the most trouble. Tina assured me, that this would improve with time. Tina also had Phill, dig through a can of beans, and find these little objects hidden in there, and retrieve them, with his left hand. They were pretty small objects, so this helped with his fine motor skills.

I wasn't sure how to describe, this new turn in our lives. One single moment, had changed everything. Here I was, standing, in a Rehab facility, while I watched the man, I had been with, for thirty-one years, as he struggled to regain motor skills. Fighting to relearn speech skills, and the ability to dress himself. I could not let myself dwell on these things, right now. I needed to put one foot in front of the other, just one day at a time

It seemed that Phill was more emotional when he laid down, than when he was working. He was afraid that we would fail financially, That as a man, he would not regain that part of our relationship. I told him, I felt in my heart, that it would all be okay. God had a plan for us. We would get through this. He told me, he did not have my faith. He was never raised with any type of religious upbringing, and he didn't know a whole lot about God. I told him, that it was okay, I had enough faith for both of us. I had read that fear of everything, was common with stroke patients. He had always been my fortress, and my protector. Now it was my turn. I would do anything I could, to help him through this.

Alisha, and Kim were hard at work strengthening the muscles in Phill's face. He tried to smile, while Kim pushed on his cheek in the opposite direction. This caused resistance, which strengthened those muscles. They then reverse it, and he tried not to let Kim pull his face into a smile. They have done these exercises from the start, and it has really paid off. We definitely, could see a vast improvement. Phill could actually smile now, with both sides of his face. It was wonderful to see that smile, and the way it lit up his face. I could even see the twinkle in his eyes.

Phill enjoyed spending time with his roommate Rick. They laughed, and picked on each other, as well as the nurses. Everyone was fair game. I loved seeing him laugh. It was hard for him to be here. He still had a lot of anxiety, and stress. Almost daily, He would tell me, that he was afraid he would die in here. I still did not have a way to relieve that anxiety. I hoped, that would pass, when we went home.

Chapter 11

Day 22

It was a beautiful day! The sun was shining, and felt warm, I knew there was a bounce in my step. This was the last day in Rehab. Tomorrow our lives would resume! I was so very happy!

Brian had a surprise for us today, in PT. We went outside. This was the first time Phill had been outside, in twenty-three days. He was so excited! Brian wheeled him outside. I knew how great the sun felt on my face, I could only imagine, how wonderful it must have felt to Phill, who had been cooped up for weeks. He was grinning from ear to ear. He couldn't believe how nice it was out. It was time to get to work. Brian started him out walking on the level sidewalk, and then moved him to a more uneven portion, to test his balance on uneven surfaces. They worked on going up, and down the curb. Brian explained where he should place his cane for each maneuver. It was so wonderful to see the sun on my husband's face, and to see him outdoors walking, even with a cane instead of lying in a hospital bed. I silently thanked God for letting me still have this wonderful man in my life. What an amazing blessing! I decided that I wanted a picture of Brian, and Phill. I took one of them, then Brian took one of us. What a beautiful picture. We both looked so happy. As we were finishing up Rick, and his therapist, Todd, came down for some fresh air. After some bantering back, and forth, Phill decided he wanted a picture of all of them. He liked the other therapist, Todd, a lot. He called him, The Mule Skinner. He named him that, because Todd had a long beard, long hair, and tremendously strong handshake. Phill thought he reminded him of a mule skinner, because of strength in his arms, and hands. So Todd became "The Mule Skinner." I took a picture of all four of them. What a wonderful moment.

I decided, I was not leaving till after dinner tonight. We had a farewell dinner with Rick, his family, and the nurses. Rick was leaving in the morning also. I had ordered some sheet pizzas, and Jenny brought cupcakes to celebrate. It was a fun little party. Jenny stayed to tuck her dad into bed, and I headed home. There was a smile on my face.

Chapter 12

Day 23

I was so excited! I felt giddy like I was going on a first date. I painstakingly took my time getting ready. I wore a sun dress that was one of Phill's favorites. I even had makeup on, which in the last few weeks, had kind of been hit, or miss. Today, however, it was the whole show for my wonderful husband! Tonight, we would get to fall asleep together, in our own bed. It seemed like forever since we had been able to cuddle, in our own bed. Could I have been happier? No, I don't think so!

As I drove to Rehab this morning, I reflected on where we had been for the last few weeks. The journey, that began on April 9, seemed surreal. I felt alive, for the first time in weeks! The sun was shining, and the air was warm. I thought, what a beautiful day to bring Phill home, and regain our lives. We had weathered the storm, and survived! I knew there would be trials, but he had improved so much. It wouldn't be long, I was thinking, and all would be back to normal. I felt so blessed.

To say that, Phill was excited when I arrived was an understatement. He practically floated on air, much like his wife. I helped him dress, and everyone came in to see him before we left. I received my orders from the doctor, and nurse about his care at home. One thing, that they had really emphasized to me, was that Phill needed constant supervision. The type of stroke he had could cause him to overestimate his abilities. That meant, he would think that he could do things that, maybe he wasn't quite ready to do. Some people, with this type of stroke, have even gone so far, as to argue that they even had a stroke. There are many, many dangers in farming, for someone with all of their faculties, let alone someone whose balance was challenged, and unaware of potential dangers on his left side. I felt the apprehension as it crept up my spine, much like the tendrils of a climbing rose. A worrier by nature, I now, had something new to focus on. A reminder of the changes that had happened in our lives. We said goodbye to everyone, and got him loaded in the car. We were off! It was so good to be driving, with Phill beside me. I felt for the first time in twenty-three days, a measure of peace. That somehow we had gained control of our lives again, and they were not spinning out of control anymore. How amazing that felt. It was like we had been caged in a dark place, and suddenly the sun shone through, sending beautiful beams of light all around us. I was so happy.

I pulled into the drive at home. The older kids are already here. Young Phill came, and helped his dad up the steps to the porch. There, hanging from the swing on the porch was a sign made of white paper plates, and ribbon. It said, "Welcome Home". Maud, Young Phill's, fiancée had made this for us. Phill was tickled with all of the attention. He was so happy to see the dogs, and especially his cat, Bear Cat. What a wonderful homecoming! After a short time, Phill was tired, so I took him in for a nap.

The rest of the afternoon was rather quiet, with the kids coming, and going to check on us. Young Phill, and Merlin, started the evening milking. I heard the milker pump turn on, and it was a comforting sound. I have heard that sound for the last 31 years. Exhaustion was beginning to catch up with me. I was ready for bed.

We climbed into bed, and cuddled for a few minutes. It wasn't long before I heard Phill, as he began to lightly snore. I was just dropping off to sleep, when all at once he startled, and jumped. His left arm had come into contact with me, and it sent an electrical jolt through him. He is now awake, and anxious. We decided to swap sides of the bed, so his left side wouldn't be so apt to bump into me, and startle him. I was okay with that. Whatever worked for him to sleep was okay with me.

Some stroke patients have their sleep patterns affected by their stroke. Phill was one of them. He was awake after just a few hours, and he wanted to talk. We talked for a couple of hours, and then I told Phill, that I really need to sleep for a little bit. He said, "Okay I'll be quiet." With that said, I closed my eyes. It was only a few minutes, and he was ready to talk again. As I mentioned earlier, one of the areas affected for Phill was his sense of time. Minutes felt like hours to him. So started our new pattern.

Chapter 13

Day 24

After chores were done this morning, Young Phill came with his Honda side-by-side, and asked his Dad if he wanted to go for a ride. They took off to go look at the fields, and the cows. Just to get Phill outside, so he felt like he was doing something. It was a gorgeous day for a ride. Young Phill was in shorts, and so is his father. This was practically unheard of for him to be outside in shorts. As they were traveling along, Phill's left hand had found purchase on Young Phill's bare leg, and was rubbing it. His dad was completely unaware of where his left hand, had found purchase. Young Phill, however, kept a very close eye on that hand.

After their ride, the guys took the big loader tractor out front to the hay stacks. We needed to see how Phill would do, operating the tractor, and loader. Jenny and I watched from the sidelines, so we could video. Phill seemed to handle the driving part okay. They started to move some bales out of the stacks. These bales are three foot by three foot by eight foot long, and stacked five bales high. My husband was always a master at moving these bales. He decided to get one of the bales higher in the stack. That would have been okay, except there was a bale lower to the ground, that prohibited him from getting the top bale safely. He was unable to figure out, he had to move the lower bale, in order to reach the higher bale. Instead, he tried to climb the stack with the tractor. Each time he tried, Young Phill popped the tractor out of gear. This infuriated Phill. He insisted he knew what he was doing. In the past I have always been able to trust his judgment. Having heard the therapists, as they told me, that he would over estimate his abilities, I was suddenly very apprehensive about how he was going to do. Was this one of those times? I was not sure.

Day 25

Phill and I made our way to the barn this afternoon, while the guys were putting cows in. He actually got to close the stanchions on a few of them, and that made his day. We spent a few minutes talking with Merlin about the herd, and how things were going. Merlin had spoken several times in the past, about how impressed he was with our cows. They were a cross between Jersey, and Brown Swiss dairy cows, which made them smaller in size, but able to produce a fair amount of milk with a high butterfat, and protein content. They were a nice bunch of cows, which had served us well over the years, and paid the bills. They were Phill's pride, and joy. Merlin told us, he had been enjoying them.

We took our Kubota side by side for a ride today. I started it up in the shop, and Phill climbed in the passenger side. I backed it out of the shop to turn around, and during this procedure, his left hand had managed to find a new place to settle. It had found its way in back of me, and is now roosting in the back of my shorts. I turned to look at him. He is staring straight ahead. I said, "Hon, do you realize that you have your hand down the back of my britches?" He replied, "I had a hold of your belt loop." "That wasn't my belt loop!" I replied. He looked at me, and we both start laughing. He said, "Do you think that I could get away with that with anyone else?" I said, "Not and live!" We both laughed again. It felt so good to laugh!

Chapter 14

Day 26

Today would turn out be one of the most stressful days of our lives. Our friend, Huck, who works for a farm service agency, was coming over to discuss what our options were to keep the farm running after the stroke. Young Phill, and Merlin had been milking cows, and taking care of the dairy since the stroke. They wouldn't be able to keep doing it indefinitely. Phill, by no means was ready, or able to take over the reins yet. I was not sure that he would ever be able to milk cows again. Let alone feed, clean, and care for over seventy animals by himself. One of the areas that was deeply affected by the stroke was his stamina. Three weeks ago, Phill was putting in twelve to fourteen hour days every day. It was his way of life. Now, he is exhausted after an hour. Huck arrived, and we headed into the studio. He had brought all kinds of paperwork pertaining to the dairy industry as it was at that moment. We had our own paperwork. Maud, Young Phill's fiancée, had made up spread sheets, that tell how much money we needed to live on for a year. It was time to talk. Huck began, by asking Phill, when he had planned to stop milking before the stroke. Phill replied, "Probably never." He said, "I probably would have died there in the barn, and she would have found me." Huck asked him if he thought that would be fair to me. He just hung his head, and said, "No". We went on to talk about the actual options open to us at that time. One, we could try to hire a herdsman. This is someone whose sole responsibility is to feed, milk, and take care of the cattle. Huck gave us the going rate that herdsmen make. It was astronomical to us. Milk price, prior to this, was the best we had ever seen in our lives. However, in the months preceding Phill's stroke, the price had dropped ten dollars per hundred pounds of milk. To afford to hire a herdsman, we would have to be paid twenty dollars per hundred. We were barely making sixteen. The other factor was finding someone to hire. No one wants to be just a herdsman anymore. If they wanted to milk cows, then they wanted to milk their own, not someone else's. It was quickly becoming apparent the there weren't a lot of options really available to us. Phill, was physically incapable at this juncture to milk cows, and do chores. He probably would never have the stamina to do this work. We talked about selling the herd, and what it would mean financially, and what we could do to keep the farm running. We could sell feeding hay, that we normally fed the dairy, and continue on with our mulch hay business. Hay, that wasn't of good enough quality, to be fed to the cows, was sold to the mushroom growers, for a mulch bed to grow mushrooms. We didn't have much left in debt. When the milk price was great, I put money away, and paid off most of our equipment, just before that fateful day. Looking back now, that had been a really great idea! Huck told us the price of dairy cows at the sales were at an all time high. We would get a good price for our herd. Phill looked at me, and started crying. "What do you want to do?" He asked. There was no way I could answer him. I could see the devastation in his eyes. We were both crying hard. This was so awful. This was the life that he had been born into. It was all he had ever known. Unless he had surgery, or one of the few vacations, he has gone to that barn every day of his life, since he was old enough to walk. I couldn't imagine what he was feeling. My heart was breaking, and this had only been my life for the last thirty-one years. These animals were more than just our livelihood. They were our babies, our friends, and our joy. They were the reason we had lived our lives the way we had, We loved what we did. Young Phill, and I had a conversation about the cows just recently. He said he did not want to be a dairyman, but he now understood what his dad, and I felt about the cows. They have distinct personalities, and behaviors unique only to them. Like for instance Grammar, when I would walk by her head in the manger I would say, "High five Grammar!" I would hold my hand up palm facing her, and she would take her nose, and hit it. There were times when I was busy, and didn't stop to fuss with her, or I was distracted, when I walked in front of her.

She would take her nose, and shove me like she was saying, "Hey I'm here"! Some of the cows would turn around, and kiss us when we were milking. Never again would we laugh at Grammar's antics, or love on these cows, as we milked them. I was at a loss as, to how this could have happened? How could life just be going along, and one day you wake up, and the entire world is upside down. Nothing made sense anymore. Nothing.

After Huck left, we were just quietly sat. Young Phill was in the barn. He came out, and said we had cows out. Phill took off headed for the truck. He wanted to go check the fence over back to make sure it was up, and closed. He started to get in the driver's side of the truck, I told him, "I am driving." He answered me, "No! I am driving, give me the keys!" I argued with him for a few moments. I was thinking of all the obstacles up back that he would need to maneuver around, and thinking he would never be able to do that! Phill looked at me with tears in his eyes, and said, "You have to let me do things. I need to do this!" I was torn. I was thinking of the overestimating the abilities thing again. I tossed him the keys, but I would ride right next to him, so I could shut the truck off, if I needed to. Phill did fine. It gave me some peace of mind, and he was right, I needed to extend his boundaries, and let him see what he could do.

Chapter 15

Day 27

It was a restless night. I had been up, and down all night, and I was certain Phill had not slept much better. When I opened my eyes, Phill was awake. He looked at me, and said, "I have to tell you something." I laid there, and looked at him. I waited for him to say what was on his mind. Finally he spoke, "Last night while you were sleeping, I decided to end my life." I felt like I had been punched in the gut. It was hard to breathe. Phill started to cry. "I made up my mind. I even planned what I was going to do," he said. He went on, "I looked at you lying there, and I knew how your brother killing himself had affected you, and your family. I decided I could never hurt you like that. I knew that it would destroy you, and I couldn't do that." I said, "It would destroy me." He looked at me, and said, "I know. I promise you, I won't do that." I didn't know what to say except, "Please, please don't ever do that." He looked down, and replied, "I won't." I knew this decision to stop milking, and sell the cows was going to be tough; I never dreamed that it would shake him to his core. Shake him enough to think about ending his life. There was no way to be prepared for this type of event. You can think that you will know how you will act, or behave, or how you will do things, but until that day arrives, and you are faced with a life that is totally out of your control, you do not know how you will act. This decision to sell the cows, he may never recover from. This was a lot to absorb. I needed time to think things through, and Phill didn't want me to tell the kids. I didn't want to tell the kids. He promised me that it would never happen. I wanted to believe him. He had never given me a reason, not to trust him. I prayed that I was right.

Day 28

It seemed we had fallen into a routine of sorts at night. We slept for a few hours then Phill would wake me, and we would talk. We talked about everything. He was scared we would not be able to survive financially. I reassured him, that I felt in my heart, we will be okay. Didn't sound like much of an assurance, but it was all I had. We would go back to sleep, at least I did. I usually told him, that I needed to sleep for awhile, and he would say, "Okay I'll be quiet." I would smile, because I knew that would last about a minute, or so, and then he had to talk some more. Eventually I would fall asleep to the sound of his voice, which sounded soothing, and pleasant to me, as I drifted off.

We got up this morning, and I got Phill to eat some breakfast. He still was not eating well. I found him subdued, and quiet. I knew he was thinking about the cows, and he just felt bad. He went back, and laid down on the bed. He laid there for awhile, not saying anything. I saw him sinking away from me, right before my eyes. If I allowed him to become despondent, I would lose him. I went in, and sat on the bed with Phill. "Come on, get up." I told him. "It is a beautiful day we are going to go do something, not just lay here." "What are we going to do?" he asked. I said the first thing that popped into my head. "Go pick rocks." I told him. I was thinking to myself, "Where in the world did that come from?" I hated that job, but he enjoyed it. He loved to see a field all picked free of the rocks that can damage equipment, when cutting hay, or raking, and baling. So off we went with the RTV, armed with shovels, and a pickaxe to dig the rocks out. We took off, and Phill drove. We spent the next few hours picking rock, and laughing in the sunshine. He looked so much better outdoors than he did in that bedroom. I suggested, when we got done, we go for a late lunch at the Red Lobster. He thought that would be great.

We were sitting in the restaurant, enjoying the day, and I began to tell Phill about a conversation that I had with Jim, our hay trucker. Jim had called about picking up a load of hay, and had told me that he would load the load, as Phill just wasn't ready to try to load a truck with the tractor. As we were talking, Jim told me about a conversation with his girlfriend, who has worked with stroke patients. Jim asked her if Phill would come back from this stroke. She said, "Will he be able to milk cows in the morning, do field work all day, then milk cows at night?" She continued, "No he won't, he will not have the stamina to do all of that." When I told Phill about the conversation, he said, "I'm so glad you told me, it makes me feel better about selling the cows" I was happy. I would do anything to make this an easier transition for him. I just didn't know that it would be this hard. I naively thought that once the decision was made, that he would accept it. I was not dealing with the man I have known for over thirty years. This was a new person, a new entity that I had just recently met, and have yet to figure out. I prayed for God to give me guidance, and to help him through this, as I didn't know how to help him.

Day 29

Today Christie, the new PT Therapist, put Phill on the elliptical. He started running it backwards, and couldn't get it to go forward. His left leg wanted to go backwards, and he had quite a time convincing that leg to go forward. Christy, and I got quite a chuckle out of it.

I took Phill to the eye doctor to see if the stroke had affected his vision. He was having trouble with disturbances in his vision, and seeing things that shouldn't be there. Christie had on a striped shirt the other day, and when Phill looked at her there were lines on her face matching her shirt. Phill also saw the bows from Young Phill's sun glasses, that were hanging on the front of his shirt, duplicated on his cheek. We were afraid that there was damage from the stroke that caused a problem with his vision. The eye doctor checked Phill out, and said there wasn't anything wrong with his vision or his eyes. What he felt was going on, was because of the stroke, the brain was processing what the eyes were seeing differently. He felt that with time this would clear up.

Chapter 16

Day 30

Thirty days have come, and gone since our lives were changed forever. We have been through many changes. We have spent time in the ICU, and in Rehab. We have made the decision to sell our dairy herd. I felt like we were afloat in an ocean, and I was unsure where we would end up. The waves pushed, and pulled us in different directions. I do not know which direction is right for us. Young Phill had ideas about the farm, and wanted to become a more active part of it. He would like to combine equipment, and farm together. I was not ready for us to make anymore life changing decisions. I just wanted some time to adjust. Young Phill understood how I felt, and dropped the issue.

The changes in Phill in the last thirty days have been many. He has gone from not being able to lift his left arm, and leg on command, to using them almost normally. He still didn't have a lot of feeling in them, as far as pain goes, however the hypersensitivity, if accidently touched, was still very great. It seemed to be compounded by exhaustion, and anxiety. Balance continued to be a struggle, and was worse when Phill was tired, or it is dark. We had to put a night light in the bedroom for him to get up, and go to the bathroom.

Phill continued to be despondent over the cows being sold. I hoped this would ease when the cows were finally gone, and we could move on. Days ran into each other, we tried to sort out what had to be done, and what we would like to do. I felt like my brain was in a fog. I thought to myself, will this feeling pass? I hoped so. I found myself feeling angry. I was angry at the situation. I was angry that this had happened, and that he had to feel as bad as he did. I tried to be understanding, and supportive, because none of this was his fault. I was not angry with him. Sometimes, I felt angry with God. Then I would remember that God has a plan. Just because I didn't know the details of that plan, wasn't a reason to be angry with God. Everything is in His time, not mine. This was hard to live by when it is your life. I looked for scriptures that helped me keep my faith. It would be very easy to lose faith, when you are faced with things in your life that turn your world upside down.

Chapter 17

Day 37

How would we get through today? I asked myself. The trucks had arrived to transport the cattle to the sale. We decided to send them to a sale, versus having an auction here. Phill didn't want to see them sold, and we felt it would be harder for him to watch them go through the ring, than to see them get on a truck. The truckers who had come all knew us. Each of them spoke to him, and tried to distract him from the events going on around him. Phill was concerned that the cows not be too stressed by being loaded, and trucked. Young Phill, and Merlin were the only ones in the barn working with the cattle. Everything seemed to go very smoothly, and quiet, just what Phill wanted. As the trucks filed down the driveway the reality of the cows being gone began to set in. We were both crying. I knew how bad I felt. I could only imagine, how bad my sweet husband must have felt. It was utter devastation. We watched those trucks, as they drove out of the driveway, our babies, headed to God knows where. Cows that were born here, and raised by us. We took care of them, and yes, loved them. Now they were gone. Most of them, hopefully would be purchased by other dairy farmers. Some, probably would be sent to slaughter, because the buyers felt they were too old, or didn't produce enough milk. We wouldn't know where our girls, ended up for almost a week. It was a very long week.

Day 38

The barn was so empty. The calves, and young stock had been taken to Young Phill's place so he could feed them, and look after them. We had some bred heifers that were pastured up behind the barn. We planned on selling them, when they were close to birthing. Phill

56

was inconsolable. Everything he had done for the last sixty years was gone. The only thing that I could do was hold him. That was all I had to offer. I felt like I had let him down. I should have been able to fix this. I knew in my head that this was not true, but my heart said something totally different. Maybe I should have taken over the milking. If I had he could have kept his cows, and he wouldn't be so devastated right now. The reality was that I physically could not have done it. I have some joint issues, and already had one hip, and one knee replaced. My other hip, had a torn labrum (liner) that needed to be replaced. I did not want to do this in the near future; however I already had trouble walking. I knew that physically I couldn't have done the milking indefinitely. I just wished I could have. Today I wished that it had been me, who had the stroke, not Phill. I felt, I could have dealt with it better than he, and it would have impacted our lives less. I tried to remember that God doesn't give us more than we can bear. I didn't know how much more I could bear.

Chapter 18

Day 41

Today was sale day. Phill was convinced that we would never make enough money to sustain us. I hoped we made enough. I relied on my faith, that God wouldn't have led us here, and abandoned us. Young Phill went to the sale as well as our friends, Huck, and Merlin. Phill, and I were killing time, as we did some small projects around the farm. It was hard to just sit, and wait. Young Phill called in to update us on how the cows were selling, and how the sale was doing. I had hoped that hearing how well the cows were selling would give Phill a measure of peace. They, at least, would give us enough to live on. He didn't even respond when I gave him the update. I asked him, "Aren't you happy with the way they are going?" He responded, "I am not happy. They are gone!" I was beginning to realize there was a possibility that he would never get over losing the dairy. What a horrible feeling for him. The only bright side of today was finding out that Merlin had bought Chubby. Merlin had sold us Chubby, as a young heifer, and she was one of Phill's favorites. Now she was back with Merlin. Chubby would reside with Merlin's cousin, who had a dairy farm. She would have a good home. Phill cried over this news, it was a relief to know, that Chubby would be taken care of.

Chapter 19

Day 45

I have to tell you a very sweet, and funny thing that my darling husband, did this morning, as we headed to the hospital, to see my mom. I stopped at the stop sign on our road, and Phill leaned forward, and said to me, "I got a Pastor, you wanna do this again?" I laughed, and said, "Is this a proposal?" Phill replied, "Yes it is! "Then yes I do!" I said. Over the years, we have often joked that he, never really proposed to me. We had been talking about getting married, and he said he was thinking maybe July. I said, "How about the fifth?" That was how we came to get married. Now I had been proposed to! We laughed, and laughed. He thought his proposal was so funny, I thought it was sweet!

The day before yesterday I had to take my Mom to the hospital. She had been in, and out of the hospital almost monthly since my father past away. Mom had congestive heart failure along with some stomach, and bowel issues, stemming from the radiation she received, for rectal cancer in 2001. Phill went with me to the hospital today. It was hard for him to be alone without me; it was also hard for me to be away from him, and wondering what he was doing. Today Mom's doctor came in, and told me they were transferring Mom to another hospital, that dealt with heart issues. Her heart was acting up, and she could have been headed into a heart attack. The hospital was not sure when the transfer would take place, and I really needed to get Phill some lunch. I decided to take him to lunch, while we waited for them to transport Mom. We no more than arrived at the restaurant, placed our order, when the hospital called, and said the ambulance should arrive in approximately fifteen minutes. Phill was ready to go. I said, "No, we have already ordered, and if we miss her at the hospital, we will just go to the other hospital, we need to eat."

He was not happy. The longer he sat, the angrier he became. He was convinced that we had been waiting hours for our food, when in all reality it had been only about fifteen minutes. When the waitress brought our lunches, he refused to eat. He was mad. I tried to gently to tell him, that it hadn't been very long, and he really needed to eat. He still refused to touch his lunch. I then told him, "It will be a long time till dinner!" He didn't care he was mad, and not going to eat. There didn't seem to be anything that I could do to change his mind, so I ate my lunch. He would be plenty hungry later I was sure.

We met Mom at the new hospital. She was nervous about being someplace different than where she was used to. This hospital was almost an hour, and a half away from home. While we were there, I excused myself to go to the ladies room. When I came out here was Brian, Phill's therapist from Rehab, walking a patient. "I didn't know you worked here too," I said. Brian explained, that he worked for several hospitals, and inquired what I was doing here. I explained about my mom, and told him that Phill was with me. Brian asked what room, and told me not to let him know he was here. He would come up, and surprise him. I was excited because I knew He would be so excited to see Brian. I was sure this would lift his mood after the lunch fiasco. It was only a short time, and Brian came walking into the room. It took Phill a minute to recognize him. He jumped up, so excited! Brian asked how he was doing, and took him out into the hall to see how he was walking. Phill had been doing outpatient therapies since we left the Rehab. There was a noticeable improvement. Brian congratulated him on his progress. For the rest of the afternoon, he was animated, and excited about having seen Brian. We left the hospital early evening for the long drive home. Shortly after we left, Mom had a heart attack. We didn't know it, until I arrived the next morning. Mom told me she was sitting there, looking out the window when the doctor came in, and asked her if she felt any pain. She told him no. The doctor, informed her that she was having a heart attack. It had shown up on her monitors. Mom told me the next day, "I almost called him a liar! I didn't feel a thing!" It was not a serious event fortunately and she would be fine.

Chapter 20

Day 48

Phill woke up this morning angry. I could tell by his eyes. He sometimes would tell me that they "looked wild", and he was right. They did look different. I knew he was upset, and I coaxed him out on the deck to eat his breakfast. He ate very little, and just stared off, or just closed his eyes. It was like he closed me out. I tried to make some small talk. Sometimes, redirecting is all that is needed to help turn his day around, but I saw that that was not going to work today. I tried to talk to him about what he was thinking. He said, "I hate this!" I said, "I know you do, Sweetie," to which he replied, "No, you don't! I WISH I HAD DIED!" He then stood up, and threw his plate of breakfast out into the yard. I felt so frustrated! In anger I threw my full coffee cup out in the yard, and said, "You want to throw things? I can throw them too!" He started to push past me to take off, and I needed him to stay here. I stepped in front of him, when he tried to push past, I grabbed his arms, and sat him down in the chair. His balance being what it was enabled me to set him down. I was appalled! What was wrong with us? We never had acted like this. I was so angry! I didn't know how God could have let this happen. I didn't know what I was doing or how to help him get through this. We both cried. We hugged, and said we were sorry. How would we ever get through this?

Young Phill, had told us about another neighbor, who had a stroke three years prior. I asked him, if he thought, the neighbor would come, and talk to Phill. I wondered, if knowing someone else had gone through, what he was going through would help. That particular neighbor came to Young Phill's, coal store by chance, that very day. He told him about his dad having a stroke, and what a hard time he was having adjusting. The neighbor said, maybe he would stop by, and visit him. He did just that, later that day. Phill was in the tractor out in the field, in front of the house, when in drove this neighbor. He climbed in the tractor, and rode around with him for awhile. He told Phill how hard things had been for him after his stroke, and how he wished many times, that he had died. He told him that, wives do not want to hear that. It comforted Phill to talk to someone who had survived a stroke. This man had been a hardworking man, much like Phill. They bulled through pretty much anything that stood in their way, but you don't bull through a stroke. It pulls the rug right out from under you, and you are left in a pile of rubble, that used to be your life. Both, of these men, who had done hard physical work their entire lives, putting in long fourteen to sixteen hour days regularly, now had trouble working a few hours a day, without resting. I was sure, his wife, just like me, also felt that a few hours is better than the alternative, death. Or worse yet, lying the rest of your life in a bed, feeling useless. I felt that he should feel lucky. Phill was not yet ready to feel "lucky".

Day 51

"Well I finally did it!" Phill said, as he stormed through the kitchen, headed for our bedroom. I followed close behind. When he sat down in the chair I asked, "What did you finally do?" "I drove the tractor into the shop with the door open, and smashed the door to pieces!" He answered. My stomach did one of those little flops, when something happens that you know can't be good. "What do you mean?" I asked. "I forgot to close the door, and I drove the tractor in the shop, and destroyed it!" "Oh." I said, not much of a response, but all I could muster, at that moment. I headed out to the shop, sure enough, there was glass all over, and a very bent, and destroyed door assembly. I took a deep breath, and let it out. Young Phill, and Maud stood there too. Maud watched it happened, and ran to get Young Phill. We looked at each other and said, "Well it's fixable". Young Phill said,

"I will call, and see how much a door assembly, and the glass is."
"Thank you", I answered. I don't know what all would needed to fix
it, and I was happy to have someone else take care of it. Later, Phill
and I talked about it. He told me there had been several times in the
last few years, that he had almost driven into the shop with the door
open. But he had always remembered at the last minute, and closed
it. This time the left side neglect, along with the short term memory
deficits, made him unable to see, or remember that he had left it open.
Consequently; BANG, the door was removed! Fixing the door added
up to almost two thousand dollars.

Chapter 21

Day 53

Phill has been going to outpatient therapy for about 4 weeks now. He saw Jackie,*(not her real name) for OT. Christie of course, worked with him for PT, and Bob was his new Speech Therapist. Of all of them, he loved Christie. She worked him hard, but there was a lot of laughter that went on between them. Christie had been focusing on improving Phill's balance. She had him hold onto a railing, and try to stand on one foot. He did better standing on his right foot, and balancing than he did standing on his left. When he tried to stand on his left, he wobbled all over the place. Christie had him do laps around the room, first he used his cane, then he tried without the cane. Christie used a belt around his waist for safety. I could see how much he had improved.

Jackie was this very young woman, who looked to be, maybe nineteen. She knew nothing about farming, She would always ask if he was planting anything. If you knew farming, you would know at this time of year, we were working on hay. But she was, as sweet as pie. Jackie had Phill search through a can of beans for the treasures that were hidden in there. Using his left hand, and a pair of tweezers, he had to retrieve his finds. It was a time consuming endeavor, to say the least. I could tell he was not happy, but he did his best.

Bob, what could I say, about Bob. He was kind, and understanding with Phill. I have known Bob's wife for many years, but I had never met Bob. One of the hardest areas for Phill, was frustration. Everything made him frustrated. If putting on his pants, shorts or shirt gave him the least bit of trouble, he would fling his arms, or kick his legs, and try to throw the garment off. Bob worked with problem solving. He used the written aids, where you have to find the answers to the questions, by process of elimination. Phill hated these to his core. These were the same aids that Kim, and Alisha used in Rehab, that reminded him of the achievement tests in school. However, having Bob administer these seemed to help. I don't think he felt as judged, as he did by two beautiful young women. Those papers still made him frustrated, but he didn't feel as stupid in front of Bob as he did with the girls. Bob spent a lot of time talking with him, and it helped to settle him down. Some days he became so upset, he cried. Bob has ripped up those papers with Phill, which helped him deal with his frustration. Believe it or not, that little act of kindness made a difference!

Day 58

Phill went, and raked hay today! Young Phill took pictures. and posted them on the Facebook page, for everyone to enjoy. It seemed so great to see him doing something that he has done forever, and I could tell he enjoyed doing it. I headed back to the house to get some work done. It wasn't long when Young Phill called me, and said, "Don't tell Dad, but when he was leaving the field, he clipped a round bale. I can see that the back flag is damaged." At this point, his dad has come in the driveway, and was headed up back. I saw him get off the tractor, and look at the rake, then he started yelling, and stomping. "Too late!," I told Young Phill, "He already knows." I hung up, and headed up the driveway towards Phill. I surveyed the damage. I was pretty sure we were going to take another hit in the wallet. Oh well, what will be, will be. Somehow, we would get through this. I now understood it would not be unscathed

Chapter 22

Day 60

Two months had come, and gone since the day our lives were changed. On one hand it seemed like time had flown by. On the other hand, we seemed to be stuck in a time warp that couldn't possibly be our life. We still had not come to terms with our, "new life!"

Phill tried his hand at mowing the lawn today with the zero turn mower. I was talking on the phone, watching him mow the front yard, and the ditch. He seemed to be doing fairly well, controlling the mower. There was a slight difference between the left, and right direction, as his left isn't as strong, when controlling the mower. He had to compensate from one side to the other. I headed into the house. I was still on the phone when I noticed the mower sounded funny. I looked out the window, and saw that he was now stuck in the ditch, and trying to get out. It was not working. I quickly ended my call, and ran out. Neighbors began stopping to lend a hand. Phill told me to go get the RTV, and pull him out. The RTV is Kubota's answer for a side by side four wheeler, with 4-wheel drive. In the meantime he was just visiting with everyone who stopped. They all were glad to see him, and told him he looked good. Phill asked me, "What did I look like before? Chopped liver?" We all laughed. I returned with the RTV, and we pulled the lawn mower out of the ditch. After we got it out, he decided to mow the ditch with the Steiner. A small tractor-like machine, that we used to use in the barn to push around big hay bales. It has several attachments including a lawn mower, and was considerably more stable. There was always a little trick, to getting the mower deck attached. Phill struggled with his depth perception, and he had trouble lining up the Steiner, and the mower deck. He couldn't get it connected right. In the process of trying, one of the mounts had gotten bent. It wouldn't allow the belts to connect right, or line up correctly. He was frustrated, and walked away. I ended up calling the dealer that sold us the Steiner. He came over, and picked it up, took it, fixed it, and brought it back. It was a three hundred and fifty dollar fix.

Day 63

This morning Phill, and I went down to the pole barn to get the tedder. A tedder is a piece of hay equipment that spins the mown hay, and lays it out flat to help the hay dry faster. It has arms that fold up in two separate positions for traveling on the road. After the nerve wracking half hour it took us to maneuver it around other pieces of equipment, and out of the pole shed. We then fought to hook up the hydraulics. we took it down by the shop where Phill tried to get it unfolded. You had to do several steps simultaneously to unfold it. He was unable to do this. Phill became so upset that he was crying, wishing he had died. I hear this daily, sometimes several times a day. It hurts for me to hear every day how much he wishes he had died, when I thanked God, every day, that he was still here with me. Phill was so upset, that he told me to just go, and leave him alone. I didn't want to, but I was upset, and on the verge of tears myself. I headed up back for a walk. I found myself enraged over all that has happened, and I began to cry. All the emotion that I had been holding back for months, came forward in a torrent of hot tears. I am unable to control them. I tried to catch my breath. I stood bent over a piece of equipment, and sobbed until there were no more tears. I felt dry. My heart still hurt, but I couldn't shed another tear. I had cried myself out.

Chapter 23

Day 66

Our granddaughter Catlin, and I were supposed to go to Ocean City MD for her "Sweet 16" birthday trip. When the grandchildren turn 16, I take them on a trip to someplace special, and we spent time with each other. So far. I have been to the training camp for The Philadelphia Eagles, and to visit the Cleveland zoo. I have taken a granddaughter to Hershey, another went to the Broadway Show, "Mama Mia," in New York City. One grandson, and I went kayaking in the Adirondack Mountains of New York. I was able to visit the East Wing of the White House with yet another grandson. This was the first time that I have not been able to take a grandchild, and do their trip. I was so sad. Catlin, and I were supposed to go to Ocean City, Maryland, with the kayaks. We were going to spend a day kayaking the salt pools that border North Carolina, in hopes of seeing the wild horses that frequent that stretch of beach. But at this time I could not leave Phill, and he would not be able to go with us, due to his ongoing therapies. His balance is such an issue that, I felt that kayaking would be disastrous. He has a fear of water that we had been working on over the last few years, but I feared now, we had worse issues to worry about. I had to ask her mother to take her. The trip was already paid for, and I felt she needed to go. Catlin, and her mom went, and they had a good time.

Today was Graduation Day for Phill! He, and Bob have decided that Phill was done with Speech Therapy. Bob felt that Phill, would learn more coping skills as time went on. He felt that he has taken him as far as he can. Phill was happy in the sense he would no longer have to take those "Tests", but also sad, to say goodbye to Bob.

Day 74

Today was Father's Day. We had so much to be thankful for, but for me, and my mom, it was bittersweet. This was the first Father's Day, without my dad.

On a good note, Phill loaded his first tractor trailer of hay since the stroke today. Jim, the truck driver has loaded his own truck since, before we came home from the hospital. Phill hadn't felt confident enough to try, until now. Jim rode in the tractor with him, and helped choose the bales to load. He was so proud of himself, but he was exhausted. The thought processes needed to load the truck had taken a toll on him. To place the bales on the truck, he needed to know, just how close to be, to set the bale on the truck, without damaging either the truck, or the bale. It required him to think about each action, and make sure it was everything lined up correctly. It took a lot out of him.

We finished off the day by celebrating Father's Day with the older kids, and some of the grandkids. It was a good day.

Day 75

Today Phill had the first appointment with our family doctor since his stroke. She showed us the MRI of his brain that was taken the day after his stroke. I was amazed at the size of the damaged area. The doctor told us that some of the injury will be reabsorbed, much like a bruise is reabsorbed. She said there will be a point of impact left. We wouldn't know till later, how large an area, or what had been affected by it. That would be the area that we would see a long term deficit in. He seemed to be coming along quite well physically. Emotionally, however he still struggled. Phill had been despondent since our decision to sell the dairy herd. Whenever he went near the barn he cried. He was unable to sleep much over a couple hours a night total.

Frustration was a factor that he has had to deal with since the stroke, but now was magnified by his current frame of mind. Daily he has told me he wished he had died. He would sit with his eyes closed, so he didn't have to talk, or interact with me. I was at a loss of what to do for him. At the hospital, the doctors. told us that depression affects most stroke survivors at one point, or another. I didn't doubt that he was depressed; he had lost everything that had been his life since the day he was born. Phill refused to take antidepressants. His older sister had been medicated for years, for a variety of mental problems. I was unable to convince Phill, that his situation was different, than Alice's, and that she was mentally ill. Phill made me promise that I wouldn't let anyone give him antidepressants. I promised him. For in the end, it is his decision. I now had to figure out a solution helped him feel better, yet isn't violating his trust. I talked to our youngest, Jamie about a solution. She told me to try Valerian Root, it was good for promoting sleep, and a side effect of it is how it affects anxiety. It was used throughout history to help alleviate anxiety. I talked it over with our doctor to make sure there aren't any drug interactions with the medications that Phill was currently taking. Our doctor gave me the green light to give the medication a try. So far we have tried Melatonin, to no avail, for sleeping. Benadryl was another option, but that ended up "wiring" Phill instead of relaxing him. I was hopeful that we had found a solution. I decided to try Valerian that night. The label said that he could take up to three capsules a day. Bedtime found Phill very anxious, and upset, as well as frustrated at the way his life is right now. Lack of sleep isn't making things any better. I made the decision to try the three based on how upset, and angry he was. He took the pills without question which in itself, was troubling for me. Phill usually fought taking any medication, and he didn't even question me, as to what these pills were. He just opened his mouth, and took them. Thirty minutes later the effects were apparent. He had settled down emotionally, and was sorry for his earlier behavior. He was sleepy. I was cautiously optimistic, this might just be the answer. His sleep patterns still remained disrupted, but he was calmer it seemed, when he woke up.

Day 82

We purchased two new iron bed pieces, to replace the wooden ones on our hay wagons. The old ones had broken over the years, and been repaired a number of times. Phill wanted the iron replacements, so that he wouldn't have to ever worry, about replacing them again, they would last his lifetime, and then some. Young Phill helped him lengthen the running gears for both wagons. It now was a matter of picking them up with straps on the loader, and setting them on the running gear. Where to place the straps became the question of the day. Figuring this out was a large pitfall for Phill. He quickly became frustrated when he couldn't seem to find the correct position to place the straps. I was trying to help, and I could see that my helping, is frustrating him even more, so I did the hardest thing that I could do. I walked away. I left him to figure it out on his own. I took my mom, and we went to town. I left him frustrated, and angry all by himself. I asked God to please watch over him, and keep him safe. When we returned? Phill had figured it out all on his own, and had the bed pieces set on the running gear. I too figured something out... that sometimes the best way to help Phill, is to not help him. It was a hard lesson. I felt I had to fix everything.

Day 83

Another milestone crossed off the list. Today we worked on the wagons again, and we, both had grease all over our hands, when Phill said, "Will you take me to town to get a bolt?" I said, "Of course I need to go wash my hands." I ran across the yard, and into the house. I quickly washed my hands at the kitchen sink, grabbed my purse, and ran out of the door. The pickup that had been parked up by the wagons where we had been working is gone. I start looking around for Phill, and the truck. I ran around the side of the house in time to see our pickup passing the neighbors house, on its way to town, with I assumed, my husband at the wheel. This was the first time he had driven, since the stroke. I gave him a little time to get there, and back and when he didn't return in what I felt was adequate time, I took the car, and head for town. I did not meet him on the way, or see any evidence that he might of had a problem. I took the street that I thought he would take, based on how he used to go, and still did not see him. It had started to rain pretty hard which added to my apprehension. He was not at the hardware either. I headed back home. When I got home, I found Phill in the bedroom sitting in the chair. I walked in close the door, and ask softly, "Why didn't you wait for me?" He replied, "I waited and you never came back!" As I have said before, Phill's sense of time had been damaged by the stroke. I told him, "I ran in the house, washed my hands, grabbed my purse, and ran back out, and you were already down by Franks's!" Phill kind of smiled, and said, "Well it seemed like a really long time!" "We need a new rule!" I told him, "From now on; WIFE WILL ALWAYS COME BACK! WAIT FOR WIFE!" Phill grinned at me, and I grinned back. Soon after this discussion, daughter Jamie called, and I made him tell Jamie our "new rule". He laughed as he told her. But I did have to admit, he must have done okay driving to town, for he made it there, and back all in one piece!

Chapter 24

Day 88

Today we celebrated our twenty-ninth anniversary. It was kind of bittersweet. We have always made a big to do about our anniversary. We have always exchanged cards, however in the last few years there really wasn't any gift that either one of us needed, so we skipped the gifts. We just exchanged cards, and went out to dinner. I was so thankful to be able to celebrate this with Phill, but the excitement that he used to have, had changed. He was going to dinner because I told him it was what we have always done. I knew he loved me, he often told me, especially when he was emotional. I think that this was all so new that we were not sure how we were supposed to act.

Dinner was great, and I saw a glimpse of the "Old Phill" He laughed, and joked like old times. We held hands across the table, and he told me I looked beautiful. He also ate well. Our anniversary was peaceful, and as hectic, and unpredictable, as our life had become, peaceful was just perfect.

Day 99

Today was Phill's last day of PT, and OT. He was kind sad not seeing Christie, and Jackie anymore, but was relieved not to have to work around therapy all the time. When we went in there was a note on the OT door that said, "Hay" Guess who is "baling" on us? Congratulations Mr. C! Phill was tickled beyond belief, that the girls had gone to the trouble of making him a sign, and using "farm words"! It made his day.

Day 101

It was hard to believe that our lives had changed so much in such a short time. Phill was now walking without a cane. He was still very unsteady, but he refused to use the cane anymore. When Phill was tired his balance became even worse, as did his speech. The other day, Young Phill came bursting into the house, and said, "You have to come! Dad is slurring his words big time!" A bolt of white hot fear shot through me, at hearing those words. I jumped up, and raced up back to find Phill. I found him hooking up to a piece of equipment. I said, "Hey, how are you doing?" He said, "I'm okay" I could hear the slurring in his words. "Okay, how about giving me a smile?" I said. He smiled, and to my immense relief his smile was equal. I also had him pick up both arms. Everything except his speech was working as it should. I let out the breath that I had been holding, and told Young Phill, "He is fine, just tired." You can't understand that fear unless you have experienced a stroke. The thought is always with you.

Today Phill was in the same mood he had been in for weeks. He cried, he beat himself up verbally, saying things, about how worthless he was, and not good for anything, along with the ever present "I wished I'd died!" I have tried everything I can think of, to help him out of this funk, to no avail. I was at a loss, as to what to do. To calm him down, Valerian had become my new best friend.

We headed to Buffalo today, our grandson Zane, had a Little League game, and daughter, Tamy, had invited us to come, and watch. I hoped the distraction would help redirect Phill from his current course of thinking. We enjoyed spending the day with the kids, and watching the game. Phill seemed animated, enjoyed talking with Tamy. I was hopeful that we had indeed redirected him, and maybe he could focus on something besides the dairy. As soon as we headed home, I found my hopes dashed. Phill became sullen, and quiet. I tried to make small talk about our day, and he didn't really answer. Finally, I had enough. I told him, if we were ever to get over this, he was going to have to climb out of that hole, he climbed in to, or we would never be able to get beyond this. I said, "It sucks that you had a stroke! But you did, and now we have to deal with it!" I was angry. "I can't help you if you don't help yourself! I can't do this alone!" He started crying. It made me feel bad, but there were things I felt needed to be said. I continued, "I am NOT going to let you wallow in self pity! That is NOT who you are! And another thing, I DO NOT appreciate you trashing the man I love! He is a wonderful, kind, and caring person, and the hardest working person that I have ever known!" He said crying, "I am so sorry! I shouldn't do that. I didn't know how it made you feel." I told him, "You got mad because Young Phill tried to help you, but do you remember who helped Grandpa?" (Who was Phill's Dad.) He said, "I used to send Kevin, (our hired hand,) to watch over Grandpa, and help him; I guess Young Phill is my Kevin." I replied, "Yes he is, and you have to let him help you! It isn't bad, it just is, what it is! I love you, and we have to get past this!" Phill assured me he will try to let things go. I was finding out what a hard road, in which we traveled.

Chapter 25

Day 103

The Steiner took another hit today. Phill tried to put the mower attachment on again, and bent another piece underneath the mower. The mechanic that worked on it for us, would take a look at it. I hoped that wasn't too bad on the wallet. The Steiner was fixed. It was another three hundred dollar expense. Phill felt terrible about the repairs. When I took the truck in for inspection, the guy who worked on our vehicles, told me, when his dad had a stroke, he had to put three transmissions in his dad's truck, in the first year, following the stroke. When I told Phill what I had heard at the shop, he said it made him feel a little better. It just goes with the territory, I told him.

We purchased some Angus beef cows, and heifers for breeding. It was a start to our new life. We sold the bred dairy heifers, that we were raising, to some Amish. We only had some young heifers, not of breeding age yet. We planned to raise them up, and sell them as bred heifers. We hoped they would bring a good price.

Phill still, could not come to terms with the empty barn, and loss of the milking cows. He would cry when he had to go in the barn. It was hard for me to watch, but harder for him, I was sure.

Day 105

Phill was able to mow, rake, and even bale hay which was a blessing! I didn't know what he would do, if he was unable to do these things. As it was, they all posed challenges, and hurdles for him to climb over. Mowing he seemed to have the least amount of trouble with, however coordinating the movement of the mower, with the start of a row did have its challenges. Everything had to swing, and line up correctly, so the fresh cut hay laid, in a row, ready to be raked, and baled. He has done this all of his life, so the repetition helped him remember what to do. Raking probably caused the most frustration. He had to rake several rows at once, all into one row. There are a number of rows in a field. He had to figure out, what rows to rake together, to make it come out even, with no odd rows left. Phill's ability to figure this out was one, of the areas he had problems with, since the stroke. It caused a lot of frustration. He would find that he had miscalculated the rows, he needed to rake. For someone who had always had this gift, to look at a field of hay, and know immediately what rows had to be raked together, for it to be right for, the baler, to not being able to figure that out, was devastating to say the least. The baler offered up a different set of frustrations. It makes bales that are three by three by eight foot long, so it scoops up the hay, then a plunger compresses the hay into slices, and forms the bale. When the plunger compresses the hay, it makes a very loud banging sound, and you can feel the movement even in the tractor. The banging sound, along with the jerking of the tractor, was extreme sensory input in Phill's brain. It was kind of like sensory overload. There was too much input all happening at once. In the beginning, it was all Phill could do, to get through baling a field. As time went on, it became easier. His brain had gotten used to the sounds, and movement. He was able to process this input.

Day 108

Sometimes in life you have to walk away from a situation that you can't change, and just trust that things will turn out okay. That was my experience today. I heard the tractor upstairs in the barn when I came out of the house. It sounded like someone was racing, and tearing up in the hay mow. I walked up back behind the barn, in time to see Phill trying to place a round bale up on top of the stack in the barn. The problem was the loader didn't reach high enough to place it. Every time he tried to put it up there it came falling back down. These bales weigh about seven hundred pounds. If they were to fall on you, there would be a good chance of severe injury, or death. A few years ago a local farmer had a round bale come off the bale spear, roll down the loader arms, and over top of him paralyzing him. This was very dangerous! Phill was so mad. He couldn't get that bale to stay up there. He was ramming back, and forth. Trying to climb the lower bales, to get enough leverage, to make the bale stay up there. But, it just kept falling down. I looked at him, and he truly looked wild. He had taken his shirt off somewhere. His white hair was standing straight up. His eyes looked wild. I was so afraid for him, and what could happen to him. He looked over, and saw me watching him. He said, "Just leave me alone!" My thoughts, and fears must have showed on my face. I was torn. I felt like, I should make him stop, but I was unsure how. Then I heard this voice in my head, that said, "Let him be, walk away." I had to trust, that the one who spoke those words to me, would keep him safe. So I prayed "Please God keep him safe." And he did. Phill finally got the bales, where he wanted them, and came to the house. He was tired. Sometimes the best choice you have is to walk away. How do you know when you should make that choice you ask? I don't know how to answer that, only to say that for me, it took two elements. The first was, the belief God would handle whatever was going on. The second was, having the strength to believe in the first, and walk away. Each time I prayed, I was right.

Chapter 26

Day 111

Hooray! Our youngest, Jamie, and granddaughter Talynn flew home from Wyoming! This would be the first time Jamie had seen her dad since the stroke. Phill was so excited to see them. Jamie is the baby of the family, and has always had a special bond with her dad. As I mentioned earlier, we are a blended family. We decided early in our marriage that "step" was not a word that we would use. Our five children ranged in age from three to eighteen when we became a family. We made them brothers and sisters. We wouldn't accept less. The younger girls have never had much of a relationship with their biological father; he was pretty scarce while they were growing up. Phill was the only Dad that they really had ever known. He gave them away at their weddings; he danced the Father/Daughter dance with both of them. When Tamy was planning her wedding, Phill told her that if she wanted her "father" to walk her down the aisle, and dance the Father/Daughter dance, he would understand. She replied, "My father **is** giving me away, and dancing with me," meaning Phill. It meant so much to him, that he cried. When they danced the Father/Daughter Dance, there wasn't a dry eye in the place. She chose the song, "Daddy's Hands," because Phill had great big "farmer" hands. Those big hands had held her close on more than one occasion.

Day 113

Today the younger girls, their families, and I headed two hours away, to an amusement park. I took them there every year, when they were growing up. We couldn't do family vacation because of the dairy, so each year when they finished school I would take them, and a couple of friends to Darien Lake. It was their reward for doing well in school. We always had so much fun. We decided to make this a yearly event with their children, and it is something that I would be able to share with them. Phill did not go. He has never gone. Amusement parks were not his "thing". So he stayed home to work on hay with Young Phill. When I returned home in the early evening, I found Phill very stressed, and anxious. I had been gone all day, and it stressed him, when I was not here. He worried that something would happen to me. This too, is natural with a stroke. Fear of being left alone. I reassured him everything was okay.

Day 115

Tamy and Jamie had the chance to see the anxious, and emotional side of their dad tonight. The kids had mostly only talked on the phone with him, and he sounded fine. The only one of the kids to witness these mood swings, was Young Phill. He has seen him on a day to day basis. Still, he does not see his Dad 24/7 so even he didn't know the full extent of his dad's emotions. Tonight, Phill was convinced that he had said something to Tamy, that had hurt her feelings. He was distraught. Much like the time in Rehab, when he felt upset over "disrespecting" me. Tamy assured him, that she is not upset, nor had she taken offense at anything he had said, but he was not convinced. He left the bedroom several times in tears, to talk to her. She finally told him she accepted his apology, and he should go to bed, because he is tired! Phill finally was able to lay down, and sleep.

Phill has progressed in so many areas. His speech was much better except when he was tired. He still struggled with balance. He could drive equipment, and successfully work the hay. We were only a little over three months since his stroke. It was still relatively new, and recovery could take up to three years. He was still learning and so were we as a family.

Chapter 27

Day 116

Today I would remarry my best friend, my lover, and the man God chose for me to spend my life with. It was an absolutely beautiful day! There were beautiful billowy clouds dotting the sky like fluffy pieces of cotton, put there, as decoration for our day. The sky was the most beautiful, vibrant shade of blue. I felt like this day was indeed blessed.

I have chosen a white sundress to wear, and found a white linen shirt for Phill. I decorated white flip flops, with sparkling blue gems, to match my flowers. We decided to have the ceremony over back in the field, that overlooks the valley. This was "our place" We had in prior years, put our camper here, so we could "escape" from time to time. I loved this place!

The kids took an archway, that Phill bought me years ago over, and decorated it with lace. Young Phill brought over small hay bales for everyone to sit on. It was perfect! The food had already been taken care of by the kids. We were truly blessed, to have such a wonderful family! The only "fly" in the ointment for me today was granddaughter, Laura, who was in Japan, could not be here. She had leave coming up in a week, and was coming home for a cousin's wedding. I was sad that she wouldn't be here, but there wasn't anything we could do. She was in the Navy, and leave had to be approved.

Danielle and Pasha, arrived from Washington D.C. I decided to ask Pasha, along with Brandon, granddaughter Amanda's, fiancée, to use my cameras to take pictures for us. We did not have any pictures from our first wedding and I was not making that mistake again. I was standing in the studio looking at one of the cameras, explaining to Pasha, and Brandon how they work, and what I wanted them to do, when all at once someone was standing right in front of me. I looked up. There in front of me was Laura. I burst into tears. She hugged me, and said, "Oh Nana, please don't cry!" This made me cry harder. They have all surprised me, by flying Laura home early. This completed my day.

We had our own "limousine", which is our recently washed RTV. This was how we would travel to our ceremony. I loved it! Phill helped me in, gave me a kiss, and we were off.

The ceremony that our Son-in-law did, was beautiful. He at one point stopped to talk about his, and Tamy's marriage. When they were first married, they talked about, how there were so many broken homes. Tamy told Steve that growing up, she, and her best friend Jessica, were the only ones who had both of their parents. Steve had to remind her that she had a "blended" family. Tamy had forgotten this, which Steve said, was a testament to our marriage, and our life. He went on to say that the early years of their marriage were easy, which was usually not the case. Steve attributed their success to the fact, they both had parents who weren't afraid to fight, or wrestle with the hard things in marriage, but were committed to the relationship. This touched us both deeply and brought tears to our eyes. Our vows to each other were spoken through tears, sometimes, having to take a moment, to compose ourselves before we went on. At the end of our vows, Phill took a moment to tell me, "I hope we have another thirty years together, as good as the last 30 were." I said, "Me too!" As we left the site in our "limo", the kids fell in behind us with their cars, horns blaring. I was sure the neighbors wondered what all of the commotion was. Our Day had been the best it could ever could have been. Having all of our children, and grandchildren here was the way that it should have been. I could not have been happier! What an amazing, and blessed day!

Chapter 28

Day 125

Jamie and Talynn flew back to Wyoming today. Phill and I took them to the airport. He cried when they left. He would miss Jamie terribly. I told him that we would see her again soon, in October. Our niece was getting married in Wyoming, in October, and I would photograph her wedding as a present. This helped him calm down.

Day 126

We were leaving for Anna Maria Island, Florida, today, as soon as I finished processing, and ordering the proofs, from a shoot that I did on Monday. It was supposed to be a short job, but ended up taking a few hours longer than it should have. If I had known that it would have taken as long as it did, I wouldn't have accepted the job so close to when we were leaving. So here we were loading up to leave at eleven a.m., instead of eight, as I had hoped.

The van was loaded. We stopped at the gas station to fuel up, and I popped the hood, so I could add washer fluid. I headed inside the store, to buy the fluid. When I came out, there are cars all over, waiting to get gas. Phill told me, "Come on, we can put it in later, we don't need it right now!" I completely forgot that I had pulled the release for the hood, so now it was being held solely by the safety latch. We drove about a mile down the road when, "smash!" The hood came up, and shattered the windshield. I was doing about forty-five miles per hour, when this happened. I was stunned. My brain was trying to comprehend what happened. I was able to recover quickly and I could see the road through a portion of the windshield near the bottom, where the hood didn't have contact. I slowed down, and pulled the van to the side of the road. I got out. Phill was still sitting in the passenger seat staring straight ahead, he had not said a word yet. He finally pulled himself together, and got out. By now we were both at the front of the van. I was crying, which devastated Phill. Since his stroke he could not handle me crying, it would break his heart. He tried to soothe, and comfort me. He told me, I did a good job steering the van off the road safely. I was trying to figure out, what we were going to do. We were supposed to be in Florida in three days, to vacation with my mom, and my brothers for a week. It was our annual trip to spend time together, as a family. I felt like I had let everyone down so I was searching for a solution. Phill helped me pull the hood back down, and it seemed to be stable at the moment. I decided we would nurse the van back home, transfer everything to our car, put the van in the garage, and drive our car to Florida. At least we had a plan.

I hadn't had time to think about the ramifications of the hood coming up, and the input on Phill's brain. We had travelled about eight hours. The hotel I had booked was another three down the road. We had encountered a lot of traffic, and at one point, came to a dead stop in the road for construction. There had been cars whizzing past us, and we whizzed past other cars. All of this was input for Phill. I noticed that he was becoming increasingly anxious. He began to jump, and startle at sounds he heard around us. I made the decision to stop for the night where we were. I gave him the task of keeping watch, for a hotel sign. It at least distracted him, and gave him something to do.

Along with us was Patty, my best friend, and traveling companion, before Phill had his stroke. We had been friends for so long that she was family. My siblings considered her, another sister. She and I went in to secure rooms. Patty would be sharing with my mom which gave me piece of mind, knowing someone would be with Mom if there was a problem.

We got ready for bed, and Phill was crying, I asked him if he was okay. He said, "No, too much input today!" I could identify with that. Even for me, with a normal brain it had been too much input! The rest of our trip down was uneventful, and truthfully rather nice. We just enjoyed the drive.

Chapter 29

Day 130

We arrived yesterday on Anna Maria. The family pretty much was all here, except my cousin, and her husband who had flights cancelled. Neither my younger brother, nor my sister were able make it this year, which bummed Mom out. We made the best of it anyway.

Phill had been enjoying seeing everyone, and he was very animated. He was the life of the party. I loved seeing him like this. In the past, when we had slipped away for a short vacation, he never was able to let go, and relax. He was only doing it for me, not because he felt, he needed a vacation. The farm was his life, and where he always wanted to be. This trip was different. Not once has he mentioned the farm, or wondered how things were going there, which was so odd for me. It was almost like, out sight, out of mind. I felt this was a gift from God. Phill was able to leave the farm, and to enjoyed being together.

Day 132

Have I mentioned, how much I love my husband? We've learned to laugh at the small things. We went to the store yesterday to buy Phill some sandals, to slip on down here, instead of having to put his shoes, and socks on. It has been in the high eighties every day, and the humidity was so high. So off we went to Kmart to buy something to put on his feet. I found a pair of sandals, with straps that go over top of the foot. Phill found a pair of red flip flops, with the strap between the toes. I tried to tell him that he couldn't stand anything between his toes! He argued with me, that he COULD wear flip flops, and they would be just fine. I bought both pairs, I was convinced that he would not be able to stand the flip flops, with the strap between the toes. We got home, and he immediately tried the flip flops on, and tried to walk. I laughed as he struggled to get used to walking in them, then he lost the left one. He walked right out of it, and didn't even notice! He just kept going. The feeling on the left side, still had not come back, so he couldn't feel the flip flop, or lack of a flip flop, on that foot at all. I laughingly said to him, "Hey Handsome, you threw a shoe!" He said, "What do you mean?" I went, picked up the errant flip flop, and showed it to him. We laughed at the ridiculousness of not knowing you lost a shoe.

Day 133

Phill always had a fear of water, while I, on the other hand, was practically born with fins. I was taught very young to swim, and water was something I loved. Our condos had a beautiful pool. I had been in the pool every day since we arrived. Phill has been content to sit on the deck, and visit with anyone who was there. My siblings told me, that in all the years that we have been married, they had never had, such a great time talking with him. Before the stroke he was more reserved, and most of the time too busy farming, to sit, and visit much. They loved the conversations, and felt for the first time, they were getting to know their brother-in-law. Another small gift from God.

Phill decided, he wanted to get in the pool with me. The stairs were wide enough to walk down easily, and the water at the bottom was about three foot deep. Phill started down the stairs, and got about three steps down, when he started to panic. The movement of the pool water against his legs, caused his brain to feel like, he was so buoyant, that his legs were going to rise up, and topple him over. He was breathing fast, and crying. I sat him down on the step above him, and there was a railing that he grabbed onto, with a death grip. The input from the water that he was receiving, was being distorted by the stroke. I sat down in front of him, and placed my knees on the outside of his knees, putting pressure with my legs, and made him feel like I was holding him down, so he wouldn't float away. I rubbed his leg, and talked softly to him. I reassured him, that he was okay, and that I was there with him. He was crying, but began to settle down. In the pool already was my sister-in-law, and Patty. They were talking with another woman who owned one of the other condos. The woman turned to Barb, my sister-in-law and said, "That woman over there is rubbing your husband's leg!" Barb looked over at us and replied, "That would be HER husband!" And laughed. She then explained about Phill's stroke, just a few months prior. Barb and Phill, both have white hair, so it was easy to make that connection. We all had a great laugh over it. Phill loved this story so much, that when we were ready to leave, he went over to the woman's condo, and thanked her, for giving him a story to tell for years.

Phill finally got calmed down enough, and actually got in the water. With a couple of tubes, he floated around, for part of the afternoon. Later, however, he experienced another panic attack. We took a walk away from the condo, and talked until he relaxed, and calmed down.

Chapter 30

Day 136

We packed up the car, it was time to say goodbye to everyone, and head home. One of my brothers, left yesterday to get home, and go back to work. We said goodbye to the remaining two, and headed off the island. I was sad to leave. We needed to make one stop, before we headed north. I needed to return the sandals I bought Phill. He would only wear his flip flops. Go figure! I had to make a left turn, to enter the strip mall, where Kmart was located. I was in the turning lane. One of my brothers was in the lane beside me, going straight through. We waved at each other. The light turned green. There was a car facing me who was turning left. I could see there was nothing coming, so I started my turn. I was now crossing both of the oncoming lanes. All at once, there was a car barreling down the outside lane. He never slowed down, or made any changes in his course, to avoid us. I could see in that spit second that he was going to ram us in both passenger side doors, probably injuring both Phill, and Mom. I stomped on the gas, and we shot forward almost enough. He clipped the back passenger side, and continued on, and never stopped. I pulled into the parking lot, and jumped out. I was a mess. I had been afraid, I would watch my husband, and mother die. I was having a hard time breathing. I cried so hard. Phill tried to hold me, and calm me down. I called the police, to report the accident, and my brothers who were still in the area, come back to help, with Mom, and be there with us. It was such a blessing to have them there watching over Mom, while Phill and I, dealt with the officer. The officer who responded from the Police Department was so nice. He gently asked me what had happened. I explained about turning left at the green light, about not seeing anyone coming, then this car coming out of nowhere, and hitting us. The Officer said, "In a perfect world the other car would have stopped, and you would have exchanged insurance information, then you would have gotten a ticket." I asked tearfully, "So I am going to get a ticket?" His response lightened the mood immensely. "Pfffft NO! He made it a crime when he left the scene, so, no you won't be getting a ticket!" He told me. I was visible relieved, and his kindness has eased my anxiety tremendously. We headed over to the car, and he asked for my license, registration, along with my insurance card. The Officer looked them over, and said, "Young Lady according to this insurance card, your insurance lapsed August 1,2015?" I said, "No I just forgot to put the new cards in the car." I didn't want to elaborate on the reason, I hadn't checked the insurance cards. I hadn't planned on driving my car, until I had inadvertently smashed the windshield in Mom's car. I figured that might not look so good for me. Two cars in one week. He checked his computer, and said, "You are certified to drive farm equipment?" I answered, "Yes." His response was, "cool!" He then proceeded to tell me that a certain Highway Patrol, in an adjoining state, would yell at me for that expired card. He made quite a joke about it. Later, when we returned home I took the old card out, to put the new one in, and noticed that this particular card, was for our truck! After we completed the paperwork from the accident, and some adjustments to the car, such as bungee cording the bumper on, we headed north. Our hotel was a good eight hours drive. We had already lost a lot of time with the accident.

It has been a very long day. Phill became increasingly anxious, as the day has worn on. I imagine that this was brought on by the accident. That was a lot of input for him to handle and my being an emotional mess must have contributed. We were about five miles from our hotel, when I saw blue lights, in my rearview. The earlier premonition of our officer seemed to be coming true. Highway Patrol pulled in behind me. He walked up to my window, and I said, to myself, "I'm too tired to deal with this!" He asked me, "Do you know why I pulled you over Ma'am?" "I have a good idea," I replied. "I pulled you over for that tail light, and when I pulled in behind you I saw what happened!" He explained. This morning after the accident, we had put a new bulb in the broken light assembly, then put red tape over it. It would at least light up red when we braked, and hopefully be seen by a vehicle following us. Which in this case, was Highway Patrol."We were a victim of hit and run in Florida this morning." I told him, "And we are just trying to get it home!" He responded, "Have a nice day!" I was so relieved.

We finally arrived at our hotel for the night. I was afraid to open the hatch, in case there was damage to the structure, and maybe I wouldn't be able to close it. Instead I climbed over the seats, to get the bags that we needed for the night. It was a lot of work! By now Phill was way beyond anxious, Between the accident, the traffic, and the stroke, he was a mess. I tried to get him settled for the night, but he was in, and out of bed multiple times. He was crying, and just way over done. I gave him his meds, including some Valerian, and climbed into bed. I tried to get him to lay down with me, so I could hold him until he settled down. We were woken up at, one thirty in the morning, by some really inconsiderate people. They were yelling, banging doors, and just being as noisy as possible. I didn't call the front desk because I wanted to keep Phill, as calm as possible, but I did tell the manager the next morning. She told me I should have called the desk.

Day 138

This was our last stop in our journey to get home. This trip home has been rough. Yesterday we drove in rain, that the windshield wipers on high, could not gain ground on. I had to pull over in heavy traffic several times. It rained so hard, that inside the car, you couldn't hear one another talk.

Mom and Patty decided not to go to dinner; this trip has taken its toll on them also. We decided that we would bring dinner back to them instead. I was so tired. After we ate, I felt sick, and shaky. I laid down on one of the beds. Phill was so worried about me. He covered me up, and went to sleep in the other bed, so he wouldn't disturb me. Phill has always taken care of me when I have been ill, and now after the stroke, it was no different. I ended up sick in the bathroom. Phill was sound asleep. I was having a reaction to the accident, and all of the stress. I was just undone. I needed to talk to someone to calm down. I called my friend, Sandy. She patiently listened, as I told her, about the last forty-eight hours, and that I am sick, and shaking. Sandy told me, "It's okay, go ahead and cry. Let it out. You have been through so much!" I cried, and somehow I felt better. I thanked her for being there for me. She replied, "Always!" I hung up and now I felt I could sleep. Funny, how God puts people in your life just when you needed them the most. Sandy and I had just recently reconnected, after many years of losing track of each other. So here, I needed a kind heart, and God had brought her back into my life, to be that kind heart. I was humbled.

Day 139

Our last day on the road, and home couldn't come quick enough, for all of us, but especially, for Phill. He was startling almost constantly, his eyes looked wild, and he was not doing so well. I couldn't get him to eat, or drink anything. We stopped for a bathroom break, about three hours from home. When Phill came out of the Men's room, I could see the damage, this trip has done, in the way he looked, and walked. As I took his hand, I said, "How are you doing?" He replied, in tears, "Not good!" We got back to the car, and I had Patty climb out, so I could crawl over the seats, to get him some meds. By the time we got home, he had settled down, and was just exhausted. I shared that sentiment!

Chapter 31

Day 141

Life had returned to normal, or as normal as our life had become, since April 9. I was back at work, and so was Phill. He was trying to get mulch hay baled up, and ready to sell, as well as, cutting some firewood for winter. The latter, was an area of concern. A year before the stroke, Phill bought a couple of new chainsaws. His were very old, and he had done the research on these particular saws, and was convinced they were what he wanted. He loved them, until he tried to use them after his stroke. These chainsaws started a little harder, than his old ones did. There was a sequence, of steps for starting them. This sequence gave him problems, along with pulling the starter cord. He would get tired very quickly, when he pulled the cord. He struggled every time he went to use them. Phill had brought up a large log, that he wanted to cut up. First he tried starting the little one and it wouldn't start. Frustrated, he tossed it back in the RTV. Next was the big chainsaw. I was in the house, on the phone when I heard it start up. It sounded like it was running wide open. I looked out the window, and saw him, as he staggered down the driveway. The chainsaw in his left hand, with the throttle zip tied wide open. I hung up the phone, and ran outside. I made him set it down, and shut it off. He was so mad at me, now because it wouldn't start. I couldn't make him understand, how dangerous that was! When I told Young Phill what had happened, he said, "Oh my God!" I said, "I know!" It could have been disastrous.

Day 145

Phill and Young Phill were finishing up the hay season. There was still quite a bit of mulch hay to be put up. Phill struggled every day with the challenges, that he faced with producing hay, but he persevered. That is, who he is. He would get mad, he cried, he would fight to keep going, and then the next day he got up, and did it all over again. There are many people, who would have given up, and just sat in a chair, but not Phill. He is a fighter. I tried to remind him, when he felt down, that as hard as it was, he just kept going. He needed to be proud of his accomplishments, and how far he has come. He would always be my hero.

Day 153

We have been pasturing a small beef herd, across the road, where we used to pasture dairy heifers. Young Phill has put his cows in with ours, to help eat up the grass in the pasture. Phill decided, to try to get the beef cows, to come to him in the field, by taking them grain. The first few times, they weren't quite sure, what to make of this human staggering around in their homestead. After awhile, they came, when they saw the bucket. We put a feed trough, in the fence, for them to eat grain out of. There were a few cows, who began to come to Phill, when we pulled in. They knew what was in the bucket, and were excited to be the first, to get a taste. We used to do this with our dairy herd, and it came in very handy on occasion, when you needed to move them to another pasture, or they got out of the fence, and we had to put them back in. Phill used to be able to call them, and the herd would follow him. He looked like, "The Pied Piper," leading his band of bovines! Phill loved this interaction, and it made him smile. I loved seeing that smile. They had become few, and far between this year. I hoped that having animals again, would help with the devastation, of losing the dairy animals. At least he would have something to take care of.

Chapter 32

Day 163

Today Phill had an appointment with our family doctor. He has made great strides in several areas, in the past few months. Phill was able to get his pants, and shirts on most of the time by himself. He still had problems with the shirts, that have small buttons. He could get his shoes, and socks on, alone. Tee shirts, and shirts that go on over his head sometimes would give him a hard time, and he would get frustrated if he felt stuck, or trapped. I saw improvements. Outbreaks of temper, and frustration were diminishing. It seemed, his need for Valerian to calm down, has improved. Instead of having to take it daily, he required it now maybe once, or twice a week. That was a big improvement. I found, he still dealt with emotions, and cried quite often. The duration of the emotional time seemed to be shorter. All in all, he continued to show improvement. The doctor was pleased, and so was I.

Day 172

Phill and young Phill continued to finish up haying. It frustrated him, that he ran out of stamina, in just a short time. He would becomes so tired, it was all he could do to walk down from the barn. Phill's left side was naturally weaker than his right since the stroke. The left side became tired much faster, than the right. When he would do too much, and was tired, the effects from the stroke would be more pronounced. Phill's gait becomes increasingly more unsteady, the more fatigued he becomes. When he speaks, you noticed that his speech, has become slurred as well. I wondered if this would ever improve.

The empty barn caused so much stress for Phill. Every time he walked through the barn, it made him cry. He missed his cows, and milking so much. Today he wanted to talk to me, about resuming milking. He would like to take the heifers, we have left, buy some more, and begin milking again. I have dreaded this conversation, and I have known that eventually it would come up. I sat down and told him my honest opinion. I said, "I have to tell you honestly how I feel. I do not want you to go back to milking. I want to grow old with you, not all alone. Physically you cannot do this work anymore, and with your balance issues it is a disaster in the making. I will not tell you that you can't, I am asking you not to." Phill looked so sad. My heart broke for him, but I felt I needed to be strong on this point. His life depended on it. He looked at me finally, and said, "Okay I won't. If it bothers you that much I won't do it." For now, I have quieted that notion. Time would tell, if we would have to go down this road again. Somehow, I think that this would not the last I heard, on this subject.

Chapter 33

Day 180

I packed our bags in the car. We were headed west to Wyoming. I was going to photograph our niece's wedding. Phill and I, were also going to spend some time with Jamie, and her daughter. We would take a couple of days, while we are out there, and drive north to see my sister, who lives about four hours from our daughter. I was anxious to see my sister. This would be the first time, I have laid eyes on her since, her car accident. I was putting bags in the car, and I heard something. I Looked around, and tried to find the source of the noise. I glanced up, and there, on the roof was my husband. He had decided, that he should clean the chimney before we leave. He used a rickety old wooden ladder to climb up on the roof. The top of the folding ladder, did not reach the bottom of the roof, leaving a void of about a foot. Phill laid on his belly on the roof, near where the ladder was. He explained that once he climbed up there, with his balance issues, he became afraid, and couldn't stand up. So he laid down. I helped him find the rungs on the ladder, and helped him down. This was one of those moments, when he has over estimated his abilities. I still have to be aware of times like this, where he has felt, like he could do something that maybe, he shouldn't do. He was scared, and emotional over being trapped up there. I called Young Phill to clean the chimney. I asked Phill, "Where is your good metal ladder?" He said, he couldn't find it. So I then, called our son Brian, and found out he had taken it home, so his dad wouldn't try to get up there. I had him bring it home. I didn't want Phill to try this again, with that old ladder.

We left, and were on our way! Young Phill, my brother, and a niece, would stay with Mom, while we were gone. This would be a treat for her, she always enjoyed spending time with them. Our first stop would be Toledo, Ohio. That was approximately seven hours from home. It would make a good day's drive.

Day 181

We headed out this morning, about eight a.m., the traffic was pretty good as we crossed the mighty Mississippi. Phill loved crossing the Mississippi River. He crossed it once before, when he was in school, and the FFA (Future Farmers of America,) went to Kansas City. I think, with age, we appreciate things we see along the journey more. I had made this drive many times, but this was Phill's first time driving to Wyoming. I was excited for him to see the fields of corn, and soybean in the heartland. I knew he would love it! Tonight, we stopped in Davenport, Iowa. There was a restaurant I wanted to take him to. It was one of my favorite places, to eat in the middle of farm country. It had home style cooking, and lots of it. I loved the look of the place. It had tractors, and equipment out in front, with some straw bales as well. Phill loved it, as much as I thought he would. On our way out of the restaurant Phill found a magazine he wanted. I purchased it for him. Later, in the hotel we looked at it, and there was a treasure hunt, they do every year. Each issue had clues, and eliminates a county that the treasure would not be found in. After reading the clues, I thought I had an idea where the treasure was. In one of my treks across Iowa, my friend Patty and I took a side trip. We went to Winterset, Iowa, to see one of the, "Bridges Of Madison County," and the birthplace of John Wayne. I had read the book by Robert James Waller, and wanted to see one of the bridges. We ended up finding four of the bridges that trip. I was convinced that the treasure was hidden in the bridge in Winterset. We would stop there!

Day 182

Phill's head seemed to be on a swivel. He was not sure which way to look. There were fields on the left, and on the right, full of soybeans, and corn. We saw farmers with their huge tractors, and combines as they worked to harvest their crops. I knew how much I loved to watch them in action, and judging by the grin on Phill's face, he enjoyed it, just as much. There is a feeling that we as farmers get, when we see the earth tilled up, and crops planted, or the harvesting of crops at the end of the season. You feel it in the center of your core. It makes you feel like no matter what, everything is right in the world. It is a sense of peace. I think more importantly, it is a love of the land, that is hard to understand unless you have worked that land, had its dirt in your eyes, under your fingernails, and blanketing your body, where it finally takes residence, in your soul. That is what farming is.

We made a special stop on our journey in Williamsburg, Iowa today. To visit The Kinze Manufacturing Plant. Phill said, he would like to stop here. He had seen ads for this place showing a tractor standing, on its nose in the dirt, pulling a corn planter, that is standing up in the air. I must say it was something very cool to see. There were grain carts stacked on top of one another, according to size that are visible from Interstate 80. We decided to go to the Innovation Center, and take the tour. Phill was so excited. It made me happy to see him like this. When we finished the tour, we explored the gift shop. Phill found a book titled "Fifty Years Of Disruptive Innovation," by Jon Kinzenbaum. I bought the book for him. After we found some gifts for other family members, we were back on the road. As we headed to our next stop, Phill read to me, from his new book. He was so excited, and I loved the sound of that, in his voice.

Our journey took us next, to Casey, Iowa. An Iowan farmer moved a fourteen foot tall, 250 to 300 hundred ton rock, one and a half miles, from a field to his farm. Phill had read this story in his Farmshow Magazine, and wanted to see this rock. With the help of my trusty

GPS, we found our way, to the farm. There was a little building with pictures, and a notebook that documented, the story of the move. Phill read everything, he found there. The rock itself, was so immense, you couldn't even imagine. He stood next to it, and I took his picture. I posed, next to the chain which was a ship's anchor chain with links, two inches thick, and one foot long that they used, to move it. I loved, that I got to share these adventures with Phill. We always looked for unique things to do, on the rare occasions, when we were able to get away. This brought a measure of familiarity for both of us.

We had one more place to visit before we stopped, for the night in Lincoln, Nebraska. We headed on a treasure hunt, in Winterset, Iowa. We drove by the house John Wayne, was born in on our way, to the park, where one of the bridges portrayed in, The Bridges of Madison County, had been moved to. We scoured that bridge inside, outside, and even underneath, to no avail. We were unable find the coveted treasure. Oh well, we surely enjoyed the hunt.

Day 183

Nebraska. When you travel through the state of Nebraska it seems like it takes forever to reach the far side. It is corn fields, and soybean fields, for as far, as the eye can see. For farmers, like my husband, it was an endless smorgasbord of tractors, combines, grain wagons, and crops. He had only read, about the size of these fields, in farming magazines. To see them in person was a dream come true. This trip has given me glimpses, of the man I married twenty-nine years ago. The excitement, as he saw, how they farmed, almost 1600 miles away, from our tiny little farm, had put a little bounce in his step. For a little, while he wasn't battling the effects from the stroke, he just enjoyed the scenery, and so did I.

We stopped in Kearney, Nebraska, for lunch. We made our way down the street, to The Pioneer Museum, that was built over top of Interstate 80. I had been there several times, when I drove my parents cross county. I knew Phill would enjoy it. He enjoyed reading, about the journeys through this area, on the Oregon Trail, but he had trouble hearing the stories, on the headphones they handed out. Since the stroke, he had problems with hearing, and understanding anything with narrative, even on television. He said, he couldn't understand what they were saying; I told him, "It's okay, just read the plaques, you will get more out of it." This was another byproduct of the stroke, and one I feared, we would be left with, in the long run. It would be okay though, it was something that we could work around. With all that he could have lost, we were fortunate in many ways.

Our landing spot tonight, would be Laramie, Wyoming, at our Jamie's place. Phill was beyond excited to see Jamie, and Tay. I was excited, myself. Jamie had always been a Daddy's girl. From the day we moved in, Jamie attached herself to this man, and claimed him, as her own. Phill, has always been fiercely protective of his girls, and even more so, since the stroke. Having come so close to death, he wanted, us all, to know how much we were loved. He hoped our kids would all have a love like ours. He worried about each, and every one of them, but especially Jamie, as she is the youngest, and a single mom.

Chapter 34

Day 185

Today we drove up the mountain, to the ski lodge, for our niece's wedding. The day was just gorgeous. The wedding was beautiful, and the scenery, beyond compare. Jamie and Tay, had to leave early, as Tay was running a fever. Phill had been under the weather himself. I think he was a little self conscious, because of the stroke, and being around a large amount of people. I tried to get him to sit with Jamie during the ceremony, but he wanted to stay at a table, away from everything. The reception was in the other half of the room. Phill wouldn't go over there, or eat anything. He said, he just didn't feel good. Now I wondered, if the altitude wasn't bothering him some. Soon, we headed back down the mountain. It was dark and I was leery of colliding with, either livestock in the road, or antelope. We did however, make it back to Jamie's safely, without any new hood ornaments.

Day 187

We were back in the car, headed to Lander, Wyoming, where my sister lives. I really needed to see her. So much had happened this year, for both of us. I almost lost her to a car wreck, and Phill, to a stroke. Sandy has lost even more. Her injuries from her accident, had been so severe. There were numerous broken bones. Her neck was broken in four places. A multitude of ribs were broken, and she had to have a finger amputated the night of the accident. Sandy also suffered a brain injury, and had a brain bleed. What were the odds, that both my husband, and my sister would suffer a brain injury only six days apart? It seemed that God, gave us blessings. We were able to keep both of them, when they could have died. I was thankful every day!

When we were close to Sandy's, she called me on the phone crying. She said, "You are walking into a mess, and I am so sorry!" I replied, "Don't worry about it! We will take care of it!" Sandy had just moved two weeks earlier, and had not felt well enough to empty boxes, and settle everything. Having the brain injury compounded the task, making it seem insurmountable. When we arrived, we walked in, and found everything right where the people who had moved her, set it down. I left our bags in the car, and set about putting my sister's house to rights. Today was about unpacking. Tomorrow, we would decorate, and make this place feel like a home. With all of the chaos in the house, I found my sister extremely anxious. There wasn't one place that she could settle in, that was not in disarray. I had found that clutter, and chaos seemed to affect both, Phill and Sandy, with their brain injuries. It make them feel on edge, and upset. I could tell Phill felt this, as he wandered from room to room, not really sure what he was supposed to be doing. As I emptied boxes, I had him break them down, and put them outside on the patio. The task seemed to calm him. The neighbors across the street came home, and Phill walked over to ask, where to take the cardboard boxes, for recycling. The lady was so nice, she told him to put them all on her trailer parked there, and she would take them with their recyclables. How nice was that? In just two days, we had most of the house unpacked, and decorated. I wished we could have stayed longer, so I could have put up food in the freezer, for her, and finished the last few rooms, but we had to head back to Jamie's, for her birthday. On the way back to Jamie's, Phill told me, when he walked into Sandy's, he felt anxious, and overwhelmed by the amount of work that had to be done. He said, "I didn't even know where to start!" I explained that it was because of the brain injury, and this is why Sandy couldn't do it alone. The two of them sat down several times, to compare notes on how they had been affected. Surprisingly the similarities between their disabilities were numerous. Both struggled with deficits in long term, and in short term memory. The lack of balance was a big obstacle for both of them, as well as fatigue. Sandy's doctor, told her, the fatigue was caused by, the brain needing to rest after the injury, and that it may, or may not show some improvement with time. It helped Phill to realize that he was not alone, and he had someone to identify with, who could understand how he felt.

Chapter 35

Day 191

Our time with Jamie and Tay, would soon come to an end, and we would be headed back east. Before we left however, we celebrated Jamie's birthday. We went to Ft Collins, Colorado for lunch, and we ended up at a corn maze, and pumpkin patch. Jamie, Tay, and I walked through the maze. Phill's legs were too tired, and he was afraid, it would be too much walking, so he sat and waited for us. Tay and Jamie, picked out pumpkins to carve for Halloween. Tay had a hard time deciding which ones were the best. It had been a long time, since we had been able, to share these activities, with any of the grandkids. The oldest two grandchildren were twenty-four, and the youngest, Tay was 6. Distance prohibited our ability, to share things like this with her, like we did with the older kids. This made the day, all the more special. We all took turns at the, "corn canon," which shot ears of corn out into a field. It was loud, but so much fun. Phill grinned from "ear to ear". At times like this, that you reflect back, and think about, "how things used to be". Phill would have been home, on the farm working, and not here to share this with me. I was thankful that he was alive, and able to be here, I hated that it took a stroke to make it happen. I really do believe, that God has a plan for us.

Later in the day we took a drive up to Estes, Colorado, and The Rocky Mountain National Park. We just drove around the park for a little while, and took some pictures of all of us. Phill loved seeing this. Maybe one day we could come back, and look around a little more, but for today we were done.

Chapter 36

Day 194

So far the trip home had gone well. We covered a lot of miles. I decided to do something different. I have always booked a hotel room in advance, so I had a stopping point. Tonight we decided to, "wing" it. We would stop, when we decided we were tired. When we felt, we had covered enough miles, we looked for a hotel. We were lucky to find a hotel, right off the interstate, in Indiana. When I booked our room, I asked about a place to eat. The desk manager told me, that right up the road, is an Applebee's, that is good. Great! We love Applebee's! We headed up this two lane road. It was only a couple of miles before we saw this sign, that announced our arrival in Michigan! That was pretty cool! We were staying in Indiana, and eating dinner a few miles down the road, in Michigan. Phill loved this! Since the stroke, I found, that Phill enjoyed simple things.

Day 195

I had driven from New York, to Wyoming, many times, and almost every time I would see, this exit for The Indiana Dunes. I have to admit, I had always been very curious, and wanted to go exploring. Phill decided that we should explore. We ended up on a beach on Lake Michigan. The windblown sand had built up the dunes over many years. Phill loved the sand, and the rocks on the beach. He has always collected rocks, whenever we have gone anywhere. He filled his pockets, as I took pictures. I could tell he was tired, it had been a long trip, but it was a good tired. He looked happy! If only I could help him stay this way. I knew that if anything happened now, at least we had this time together. Looking at him, as he walked around out here, you would never know, he had had a stroke. His balance was a little off, but you might have attributed it, to the uneven terrain. God gave us blessings, in ways we would never have imagined; the sun that shone on Phill's face lighting up his smile, the wind that blew through his beautiful white hair. The biggest blessing of all, was being able, to share these memories with him.

We were back on the road for the final leg home. Phill turned to me and said, "Have you seen my wallet?" He continued, "I can't remember what I did with it." I answered him, "I am sure it is somewhere in this car." I made a mental note to look for it when we got home.

I looked back on our trip home, a couple of months ago, from Florida. Phill's ability to adapt seemed to have improved. The traffic didn't seem, to overwhelm him, like it did in August. I took that, as an indication of the healing going on inside his brain. Improvements like these, though not as easily noticed, as in the first month, were still there. I just had to look for them.

Finally we pulled in the driveway. It felt good to be home. Phill and I, worked to unload the car. When the final bag was in, we started looking for Phill's wallet. "It's not here," Phill told me. So I began my search of every bag, every pocket, every nook and cranny, that it could have been stuffed, or fallen, to no avail. It was not here. Panic immediately began to set in, for both of us. Phill was beside himself, blaming his memory, and his brain for it being lost. I calmly told him, "We will find it, don't worry!" Inside, I was not so sure. Sleep would not happen, for either of us, unless we solved this mystery. I began calling the hotels, where we had stayed, for the last few nights. On my second call, I talked with the manager of the hotel in Lincoln, Nebraska, where we had stayed our first night on the road. She said, that no one had turned anything in, to lost, and found, but she would check with her staff. About fifteen minutes later, the phone rang, and it was the manager. She had Phill's wallet. She personally went, and checked the room that we had stayed in. She found it under the bed, where it must have fallen out of his pocket, when he changed his pants. She would send it to us. It renewed our faith, that there were still good people, in this world. We felt such a relief, to have found out where his wallet was. Phill, would now, be able to calm down, and rest, which meant I could now rest too.

Chapter 37

Day 202

Today marked the one year anniversary, of my dad's passing. It didn't feel, like it had been that long. I missed him, and I knew my mom did. It sure had been a hard year for our family. I knew that Dad watched over us from Heaven, and I knew his pain was gone. Dad's best friend died a few months before Dad, and I could almost see the two of them, having a blast up there.

We drove to Syracuse to see my hip doctor, who did a resurfacing of my right hip in 2009. He sent me a letter, and informed me, there was a recall on the components used, in my right hip. At this time, I wasn't having problems with the right hip. The left hip however, gave me constant pain. I was not able to walk far, or get up from a chair, and walk without waiting a moment for the hip to work. I planned on discussing this with my doctor this morning. The x-rays of the right hip showed that the implant was in place, and there weren't any problems with the surrounding tissue. That was good news! When we talked about the left hip he told me, because I had a tear, in the labrum, there were two options available, to me. One, he could try to fix the tear, or remove the labrum, leaving bone on bone, in the joint, or do a total hip replacement. The option of having the hip resurfaced, was no longer available. The company who made the components, had pulled them off the market. I was so upset! I had such good luck with the resurfacing, and the recovery time, was less than the THR (Total Hip Replacement). The other factor, I considered was, how active I was! I needed to be able to get down on the floor, to photograph little ones, and be able to get back up. I had to have an MRI of both hips, and then we would talk about options. I was really torn.

Day 215

We headed to Maine, to spend a few days with Phill's sister, Beva, and her husband. Steve, since his heart attacks, six days before Phill's stroke, had also developed a stomach problem, that made it almost impossible, for him to eat. We hoped our visit would cheer him up. This episode had been very depressing for him. It would also be the first time Beva, had seen her brother, since his stroke. I knew she worried terribly about him. I was sure some of her fears, would be alleviated, by our visit. Beva would, also be teaching me to needle felt, a craft that she taught.

Phill did well on the drive up. He was a little tired, and traffic bothered him some, but he was able to work through it. Brother and sister, were so glad to see one another. There were tears shed on both sides. We stayed for three days, and Beva taught me so much, in a short amount of time. Phill spent his time, visiting with Steve. It was a great visit. We decided to take the drive home through Vermont, instead of going back, by way of Massachusetts. There was less traffic, and a much more scenic route. It was a great trip home.

Day 226

Happy Birthday to my love! Today was Phill's seventy-first birthday. The older kids came by, and we celebrated with cake, and ice cream. We were blessed by the fact, we even got to have this day, with Phill. It could have been so different, but we were, eating cake, and ice cream, laughing at each other, as we enjoyed being a family.

Chapter 38

Day 230

We went to Syracuse this morning, and had the MRI of my hips. We met with my doctor, afterwards to hear the results. The resurfacing on the right was good with, no issue at this time. The left however, needed to be replaced. I told the doctor. we would let him know, what we decided. It was not an easy decision for me to make. There were so many factors, to be considered. I had both Mom, and Phill to think about when deciding, what to do. I couldn't face the dilemma right now. I had too much on my plate. It would have to wait, till after the holidays.

Day 232

Thanksgiving Day! The kids would all be here, except for Jamie. She was so far away, and holidays were shared, with Tay's dad. So I would have to be content, to have four out of five, of our children. Without the dairy chores to do, Phill was able to help me with the dinner setup, and preparation, something, that I was kind of looking forward to doing together. I felt like, we were starting some new trends, to be enjoyed in our future.

Everyone was here. Steve, our son-in-law said a blessing. We had so much to be thankful for. As I looked around the table, I was amazed, at this wonderful family that we have created. I thanked God for each, and every one of them. Phill was understandably emotional today, but was holding on pretty well, for the circumstances. We got to sit, and visit, while the grandkids cleaned up. That was the deal-I cook, they cleaned up. It worked for me.

Day 234

It was my birthday. I Usually was excited, about my day. I thought maybe, I was feeling the effects, of the past seven months. I felt drained. It was like, being trapped in a hamster wheel going round, and round, with no way to climb off the wheel. I had been spinning in circles for so long, I was unsure which direction, I was supposed to be headed. I had to believe, this would pass.

The kids came by with cake, and ice cream. Phill had bought me some candy, and a card. They were beautiful cards. We started a tradition years ago of giving each other, a card for special occasions. Then it progressed to two cards, one serious, and one funny, or racy. Over the years they became something, the grandkids joked about. Who had the nerve, to read them out loud? Usually it was Brian Jeffrey, who put everything he had in to reading them, bringing lots of laughs from the rest of the kids. This made Phill laugh, and laugh. In spite of everything this last year, and as hard as it's been, there had definitely been some wonderful moments like this. I needed to remember those times, and know that it would be okay, in the end.

On a good note, grandchildren Zoe, Zane, and Aidan helped me bring in the Christmas tree. Usually I struggled to do it myself. After we got it all set up, Zoe helped me decorate it, and it turned out beautiful. Zoe has a quiet artistic inner light, that shone in the way, she painstakingly placed ornaments, and snow on the tree. Watching her work filled my eyes with tears. She is such a loving child, and made you feel, that you were the most special person, in her life. I felt that now. In a year, where I have struggled to find my footing, this was a wonderful moment. Now, when I looked at this tree, I would be reminded of this day, as I watched Zoe, help her nana, in more ways, than she knew.

Chapter 39

Day 239

Because of our new financial situation, I had the idea to make our own Christmas gifts this year. We used to make gifts, when the kids were younger, but as adults with families, it seemed like an insurmountable task figuring, what to make for everyone. This year however, I had a plan. We had to do some major repairs on the dairy barn this past summer, which required pulling off some of the barn boards. They were beautifully weathered, and rustic looking. I decided we could make wreaths, like picture frames, for the girls decorated greenery, old barbed wire, and ribbon to hang on their doors. Our sons would get their house numbers, made by hand, out of rusty old barbed wire, mounted on a barn board plank. I was excited! Phill wanted to help me, with the frames. The corners would have to be mitered, together. He had problems figuring out how to cut them, and became frustrated as he tried to get it right. I ended up figuring it out, and showed him how we needed to do it. He lost interest in sawing them, instead I got them mitered, he helped me glue, and nail them together. They weren't perfect but they looked great. Phill, then cut small pieces of barbed wire. And made staples, that held the wire in place. He did such a fantastic job! He was so proud of them. I would rather have him happy, at another task, than upset over the way his brain worked, when he tried to do something, that he maybe, wasn't ready to tackle yet. I knew the girls would love these, their dad worked, and helped create them. The house numbers turned out wonderfully also. I bent the wire to form the numbers, and Phill made staples, and attaches them to the boards. They looked so rustic. I loved them, so would Brian, and Young Phill.

Day 248

We made the decision to put the beef cows in the barn, in stanchions. Our water source for the house, comes through the barn. Putting the animals in the barn would help insure that the water didn't freeze. The heat from their bodies would keep it warm enough, and keep the water running. We planned to dig up the line this summer, and bypass the barn, so we could shut off the line to the barn. The line to the house, would be buried deep enough, to keep it from freezing. We would see how it went this winter. I decided that, maybe having livestock in the barn, would seem more normal for Phill, and help him recover, by doing the work, he had done all of his life. He wouldn't have to milk, but he would have to feed grain, and hay. There would be cleaning, and bedding to do besides. I was not sure how, he would manage physically, but I felt we had to try to ease his pain. this was the only way, I knew how.

Phill brought up four young heifers, that have not been put in a stanchion before. We had done this procedure, with new heifers, too many times to count. What made this time different, was Phill's condition. In the past, we found using gates to guide them in, worked well. Phill had been trying to get the heifers in, without using the gates. He had managed to get two in stanchions, but not without a struggle. He was exhausted, and frustrated. It didn't work the way he wanted it to. Phill was a master at moving cows, now it seemed he had forgotten, what to do. He remembered parts of what he used to do, just not the order, in which he did it. I finally called Young Phill. He came up, helped him set up gates, and stanchion them. It was the same, the next time he tried to stanchion some heifers. He became so upset, he again wished he had died.

Day 252

Phill and Young Phill, worked today to adjust the stanchions, to fit the young cows that weren't as large, as the dairy cows. It was a time consuming job, but in the end, would make putting the rest of the herd, in much easier. Phill needed help to do this. It was quite physically demanding, as he tried to get the pieces apart, and readjust them. It took most of the day to complete all the stalls, we needed, for the cows to come in.

Day 253

It was quite a battle, but we got all the cattle in the barn for the winter. They would be warm, and dry. It would also be a time, for them to get used to being worked around. Phill worked at settling them, and making some of them his buddies. He once again, was smiling. He had a reason to go to the barn. I hoped we had crossed another bridge, and were headed, in the right direction.

Chapter 40

Day 260

Christmas Eve. Tamy, and family came from Buffalo for the holidays. We were happy to have them here. She and her dad, have a special bond. She is the more rational thinking child, and was able to talk to him about things that troubled him. When he was in the Rehab, Phill told her about the conversation we had, and the "pat" answers. Tamy had the forethought, to ask him what he wanted us to say. She told him to think about how, he wanted us to answer those types of questions, and to let her know, what he decided. One night, while Phill was still in Rehab, and Tamy was home with us, He called, and said, "I want to talk to Tamy." So I gave her the phone. He told her, "I want the pat answers." She repeated it back to him, and he said, "Yes." Tamy hung up, grinned, and said, "Dad wants the pat answers!" She then proceeded to tell me their conversation. She was able to be "matter of fact" with him where I was too emotionally involved, for that. Phill was in his glory to have them here with us for Christmas. The kids were a great distraction, and always good for a laugh. I felt happy.

Day 261

Merry Christmas! As we got around, ready for brunch with the rest of the family I thought, how very blessed we really were. I found tears hiding, and waiting for a chance to escape. We had been through so much. The future, was still pretty uncertain. But there was one thing I was sure of; God was with us every step of the way. He has a plan. I just would have to trust him.

Phill was so excited! Without anyone's help, he had been able to buy Christmas presents for me. He had a gift card for Duluth Trading, and he called and ordered gifts for me. Jamie called him to see if he needed help with gifts for me, and he told her quite proudly, that he had it covered. He managed to purchase a gift at an Amish store, that I drove him to. I waited in the car, while he went in. He returned with the gift double bagged, and a huge grin on his face. It made me smile. I have to tell you about my husband's gifts in past years, and how wonderful they were. One year he picked up a rock on the farm. He spent a lot of time polishing, it until it shone. Then he made it into a beautiful necklace for me. That was the very first piece of jewelry, he made for me. Since then, there was a pendant necklace, he whittled from a piece of Black Walnut. I received so many compliments, on that piece. One year, he gave me earrings, and a necklace made from Rose Quartz. He shaped them on a tile saw, one arm in an immobilizer, from shoulder surgery. It was a wonder he didn't lose a finger! Another year, he made me a set of earrings to go, with the Black Walnut pendant. I promptly lost one, the first time I wore them. I was devastated. This was the first time in years, he hadn't been able to make me a gift. It made him sad, but I told him, it was okay, we have the rest of our lives, together.

I have to admit, I was excited also! Besides the gifts we made for our children Mom and I, made goody bags, for all of the older grandkids. We filled them with Eggnog Cookies, Monkey Bread, Cream Of Broccoli Soup, along with candies made from chocolate, and pretzels. The bags overflowed with special treats. The grandkids were happy! We had a wonderful day spending time with most of our brood. We missed our Jamie, and Tay along with granddaughter Laura.

Day 263

The barn where we housed our new beef herd, is a 200' long dairy barn, able to house over 70 animals. Our beef herd was about half that size. They were in stanchions on one end, leaving the opposite end empty. That was too large, an area for those few cows, to heat with body heat, and keep warm. Phill decided to put up a canvas at the halfway mark, to separate the two halves, so only one end was kept warm. For him to put up the canvas, it had to be cut in certain places, to fit around the beams, in the ceiling, and stanchion line. Phill had tried before Christmas, to figure this out. He was unable to see what must be done, to make it fit. He was upset over this. He headed up to again, this morning to try, and tackle this project. I could see the defeat, in his face before he even started. After he headed out I asked Steve, Tamy's husband, to go up, and help Phill put up the canvas. Steve had a knack for figuring anything out like that. He has a very analytical mind, and enjoys projects like this. It was a good match. Phill also wouldn't feel inadequate, with Steve helping him, like he did when, Young Phill helped him. It was that whole "father-son" thing with the two of them. It didn't take long, and the job was done. Phill was happy with the way it turned out. It was a good call!

Chapter 41

Day 275

The holidays were finally over, and after a brief stay in the hospital, we had Mom back home. Life was back to "normal." Our life continued on this new path. Now that we had the beef in the barn, Phill had to go to the barn every day, and take care of them. Some days it was a struggle for him. It took every ounce of his physical strength, just to complete chores. I could not imagine what it would have been like, if we hadn't sold the dairy. These chores before the stroke, wouldn't have seemed like work to Phill. He would have had them done in a matter of minutes. Now, the task felt monumental to him. It took him more than a hour just to feed grain, and hay. Part of it was, he wasn't able to move as fast as before the stroke. If he hurried he fatigued faster. The other factor was, he loses focus very easily, and sometimes moves on to another task, before the first one is finished. There were times, he was feeding, and decided that he needed to clean the barn. Before he was finished feeding hay, he would go get the tractor, and spreader. This was a byproduct of the stroke. It was something he faced frequently and we had to deal with it. He was easily distracted. He did however, seemed to be happier, since the cows were put in the barn. I think it made him feel, in a world that has been turned upside down on him, these were familiar tasks. He acted more like he was at peace. I was so thankful for that.

Day 286

The time for making the decision about my surgery has come. I have wrestled with this problem, for a couple of months now. It was not just the fact, I needed the surgery, that I struggled with. I had to consider that I was a caregiver for two people, when making that decision. Who would stay with Mom? That worried me the least. I knew I could easily work that out. My biggest worry was how to help Phill cope with this. I tried to talk to Young Phill about my concerns, but he was unable to comprehend what my dilemma was. He still didn't understand the changes in his dad. The hospital where the surgery would take place, was two hours away from home. Phill couldn't drive that far alone, and it was downtown in the city, with a lot of traffic. I didn't feel comfortable putting him up alone in a hotel. He might or might not remember, how to get to the hospital from there. I noticed that Phill's sense of direction is off, since his stroke. There have been several times when traveling, he felt we were going the wrong way. This scared me most of all. What if he got on the highway the wrong way? Not to mention most of the streets around the hospital were one way streets. This was a disaster in the making. To leave him home for the three days without me, was not an option either. His stress levels increased, and he becomes very upset, and agitated when I was away from him for even a day. I couldn't imagine how it would be for him, to go at least three days without seeing me. He would be a basket case. So, I would have to figure this out on my own. The older two daughters, had jobs, and prior commitments. Jenny could bring Phill, to Syracuse, only one day. Tamy, and her husband, would be on mid-winter break, with their kids in California, during my surgery. Jamie, offered to come out the day before surgery, and stay till I was home. She would take her dad back, and forth to the hospital, and make sure her grandma was okay too. At least I had a plan. The surgery was a go. Now I could get ready, and prepare food that we could warm up, while I was recuperating. We would get through this.

Now, the decision was made, and it was a reality Phill became more stressed. He had always been a worrier, about my surgeries. The effects of the stroke, magnified those feelings. He was not sleeping well, and was up several times a night. Phill was very emotional, and told me often, he was scared that something would happen to me. I tried to reassure him, it would be alright. It was hard to convince him, when I was unable to convince myself. This was the first time, I had such reservations. I thought that it was because I didn't want the THR, I wanted the resurfacing, and it was not available. The only reason that I was going ahead with it was because I had such faith in my surgeon. When he told me, I would have the mobility I needed to work, I would have it. He would make sure of it. If I thought I could get through another year, with this hip, work, and do the things I wanted, I would scrap the surgery, and just carry on. I knew, this is not an option, for I was having trouble, just walking, on a day to day basis. It had to be. So I was resigned to having the surgery.

Chapter 42

Day 307

Weather was a factor in Jamie's travels, home for my surgery. Instead of flying in to our local airport, and driving to Syracuse together, she was rerouted to fly into Syracuse, so we drove up, picked her up at the airport, and stayed overnight. Jamie's flight was late. She was glad, when she finally made it. She had been traveling, since early this morning. It had been a long day for her. We had dinner, and chatted, then turned in early, as we had to check in at the hospital, at 5:30 in the morning. I doubted I would sleep much.

Day 308

I tried not to be apprehensive, I knew how it would affect Phill. I just prayed all went well, and I could go home, in two days. I saw my doctor before I was wheeled in, the anesthesiologists, who would be with me during surgery, came in to talk. After I talked with them, I was confident, I would be in good hands. I have a problem, with some medications, and anesthesia. I have vomited so hard after a previous surgery, I caused a leak, where they had administered spinal anesthesia. It caused a spinal headache for days, before we found out they could do a procedure called a, "blood patch" for it. That was where, they draw blood out of your arm, and inject it in the puncture site, where they administered the initial spinal anesthesia. A spinal headache is not like a regular headache. It makes you vomit, just from pain. I never wanted to experience that again! We discussed my options, and I was relieved, to have them taking care of me.

After surgery was over Jamie took Phill, and headed home. The weather was still bad, and I would feel better, if they headed home before it got any worse. I was fine. Actually, I felt pretty good, all things considered.

Day 310

I hoped to be discharged today. I was holding my own. Yesterday, was not so good. I felt awful most of the day. Phill and Jamie came, and stayed for a few hours, then left for home. The roads were still, not good. I felt terribly weepy. I did not want Phill to see this, I knew how it would upset him, and make things worse. After they left, however, I had a meltdown. I called a friend of mine, Audrey, and cried on her shoulder. She said "I have never seen you like this!" It made her feel sad. We talked about everything for a few minutes, and when we hung up I felt better. It was only a few minutes later, when Aud's daughter, Tracy, called to check on me. She prayed with me, and gave me a large measure of comfort. I felt blessed to have such good friends.

Jamie and Phill, arrived to take me home. I was afraid this might get pretty interesting, trying to get me in the back seat of the car. It would stress Phill, too much to ride in back. Too much input. So I would ride back there. Jamie went around to the other side of the car, reached under my arms, and slid me across the seat. It was not without some pain. Jamie said, "I'm sorry Mom, I know that that hurt!" She was right, it did, but I would survive. It was a long trip home, and by the time we reached there, I just wanted to go to bed. I would need help getting in, and out of bed, for a few days. I was glad Jamie was here. Phill was glad to have me back home, and fussed over me, like a "mother hen."

Chapter 43

Day 313

Jenny took Jamie, to the airport to fly back to Wyoming, today. I missed her already, and so did her dad. Having her come, was a Godsend for us. Phill was able to handle my surgery, with her help, pretty well. We would now, have to keep track of my meds ourselves. I was unable to remember, when I last took my pain pills, so Phill moved them, into the bathroom, where I couldn't easily get to them. He wrote down the date, and time, each time he gave me a pill. I Looked at how far he had come! It gave me hope, someday down the road, he could recover a good share of what, he had lost. He did his best, to take care of me. I worried about how this would go, but now I felt less apprehensive, about my recovery. I was sure we could handle it. It was a great feeling!

Day 314

We lost power early this morning. For the majority of households, this would be a minor inconvenience. In our case however, it could become life threatening. Mom is on oxygen 24 hours a day. She has a large oxygen concentrator, and also a portable one for travel. We keep a few tanks, for emergencies such as this. The tanks were good for about one, and a half to two hours. The portable concentrator would last, about the same. When the power went out, in the night we used up the tanks, we had here. Now, the portable, was almost exhausted. Phill had to hook up the generator we used, when we had the dairy. We had to keep the milk cold, in the bulk tank. He had trouble getting it hooked up, so Young Phill brought his tractor up, and they got the generator up, and running. We now had limited power. Mom could run the concentrator, for her oxygen.

I was resting in the bedroom, when suddenly Phill came banging into the bedroom, headed for the bathroom. He said, "You aren't going to be very happy with me!" Those words gave me a sick feeling, in the pit of my stomach. I made my way to the bathroom with my walker, and saw what we were dealing with. Phill turned on the water, letting it run over, the middle finger on his left hand. Blood began to run down the drain. A lot of blood. I could see, a deep gash that ran, in a c-shape, around the second knuckle. Being on a blood thinner, made the bleeding heavier, than normal. I applied pressure, to the finger, in an effort to slow the bleeding, so that I could put a bandage on it. I finally have it slowed enough, I felt, to apply the bandage. I put two large bandaids around the knuckle, and hoped I secured the sides, of the gash together. Within minutes, blood seeped from underneath, the bandaids, and dripped off his finger. I removed them, and looked to see what else I had, to bandage this injury. I decided to try some Tegaderm, a bandage that was clear, but resembled and acted like skin. I figured it was worth a try. Phill did not want, to go to the ER. I told him it needed stitches, but he was adamant, he didn't want to go. I hoped this worked, otherwise I was out of options. You could see after I applied the Tegaderm, it was not holding. Blood seeped out from, underneath the bandage. I told Phill, we had no choice, he had to get stitches. However, I could not drive him. That posed a new dilemma. I had to call Young Phill, to take his Dad, to the ER for stitches. He had been dealing, with the effects of the power outage, at his coal business all day. I told him I was so sorry, but there wasn't anyone else. He came, and picked him up, and brought him back several hours later, with six stitches. Phill tried to cut a piece of baler twine, that was suspending a water pump out, in back of the barn. The pump had quit working, and he wanted to take a look at it, to see if he could fix it. He had to lean towards the pump, to avoid stepping in the deep water, which put him off balance. At this point Phill's left hand, had come up to balance him, and he had no idea, that it was there. When he swiped, to cut the twine, the knife continued on, and collided with his left hand, slicing around the middle knuckle. He felt no pain, he had no idea, until he saw the blood. Phill knew that I have a hard time, when he gets hurt. I feel hurt inside, when he hurts.

Chapter 44

Day 321

Today was my first post-op appointment, with my doctor in Syracuse. Jenny would drive us. Phill wanted to drive us, I told him that, I had already asked Jenny to. I knew that he was not ready to drive that far, and I was unable to, at this time. He was not happy about being driven around.

I tried my hand, at using just a cane today. I brought the trusty walker, just in case I needed it. We had to stop on the Thruway to use the facilities. I used the cane to walk in, and back to the car. I was so tired.

The doctor said everything looked great, and to keep up the good work. It was just two weeks, and I had progressed really well. I wanted this to be over with. By the time I walked back to the car, I was done in. We stopped for lunch right around the corner from the doctor's office, at TGI Fridays. I walked in with the walker.

Jenny loved spending time with her dad. She took a picture of them together, and posted them, on her FB page. They picked on each other, about their lunches. I could see, Phill enjoyed himself. We stopped at Wendy's on the way home, and got a couple of Frostys. Jenny made the trip fun for both of us, and I appreciated that. Jenny's antics made him feel like she came along for the fun, rather than just a driver. That was an important achievement, to be able to help someone, without damaging their dignity, or self esteem. Since his stroke, Phill's self esteem had been very fragile, and to have Jenny boost his spirits like she had, kept his self esteem intact. That was a blessing!

Chapter 45

Day 338

Phill had another appointment with our family doctor. We were a little over eleven months out. He didn't need to use the Valerian Root, near as often. The doctor felt he was less emotional, and I agreed he had made progress there. She also felt, for what he has been through, he had come a long way. After listening to his heart, and lungs, she commented, everything looked good. I was relieved. I kept getting the feeling, that something was not quite right with Phill. I guess I was worried about nothing.

Day 339

We celebrated Mom's eighty-seventh birthday today. I decided to do an open house. It had been four weeks, since my surgery, and I am not moving too badly. I felt I could do this. My cousin, and her husband, came over to help me prepare food, and set everything up. What a Godsend they were! More than fifty people filed in, and out, visiting with Mom, and with Phill. He had a ball talking with people, he hadn't seen, since the stroke. This afternoon I could tell he was pretty tired, and told him it was okay to go rest, so he did. Mom was exhausted also. It had been a wonderful day, seeing friends she hadn't talked to, in years. One of her dear friends, stayed after to help me clean up. I was so thankful, for my leg was letting me know, that it was unhappy with me, but it was for a good cause.

Day 341

The nurse who took care of Phill in ICU following his stroke came for a wedding consultation. Phill had not seen her, since he left ICU. He couldn't remember what she looked like, only that there was some kind of joke about, "grilled cheese." Renni had read an article, while she was sitting with him, in one of the magazines that said, people who eat grilled cheese have more sex. We laughed, and laughed, because Phill's favorite sandwich was grilled cheese! We explained the joke to him all over again, and he laughed and laughed a second time. Rennie was impressed with Phill's improvements. He had come a long way, since she had seen him. I was sure that it was nice for her, to see progress, in her patient. Most of the time, patients move on, and you never know the outcome. Rennie told Phill that he had to come with me to her wedding, because she wanted a dance with him. I found this, such a touching thing, for her to do. It made him feel so special.

Chapter 46

Day 345

It was a rough day. There was a communication problem between Phill, and Young Phill. Young Phill hadn't been able to understand, or accept the changes in his dad. I knew that it was hard. There were parts of the man that we loved, and had known, that had changed. That was the hard truth. The way he used to do things before, may not be the same now. It wasn't wrong, it just was. Sometimes a person has to look beyond the obvious, to see what is right in front of them. Our son was used to the way, his dad did things, before his stroke. It was how he was brought up. He had a hard time, adjusting to the differences, that were now a part of Phill's life. In his inability to understand, he tried to convey, how he felt things should be done, he came across to his dad as bossy. Phill felt inadequate, and pushed out. Phill had become very sensitive, towards Young Phill. The stroke left him feeling inadequate, on so many levels. His son telling him, that the cows needed more hay, sounded like Young Phill didn't think, he did anything right. He took everything personally. On the other hand, Young Phill didn't know how, to temper his words, and thought, being tough was what was needed. He felt, if he pushed his dad, he would do it the way, that he used to. In fact, all that he needed to do was lead, by example, not push. Phill couldn't see any difference in the way he did things, because of the stroke. It hurt, and frustrated him, when he couldn't understand, why Young Phill talked to him, like he did. Phill was afraid, Young Phill would take over, and take it away from him. The reality was he was just trying to help him. I hated to intervene, between father, and son, but I had to diffuse the situation. I told Young Phill, from now on, if the cows needed hay, to tell me, and I would deal with it. I could help Phill, with these chores, like we used to do together, and he wouldn't feel like, he had done something wrong. I did not want their relationship, to be damaged, from a lack of communication. I also would not allow anyone to inadvertently, cause him any more pain, than he had already suffered.

Day 350

Phill had all kinds of therapy. He had PT, OT, and let us not forget, Speech therapy. There was one more kind of therapy, that has brought about positive results, on a more emotional level. The love between a stroke survivor, and their pet. Almost three years ago, we saved a dying kitten, been born to, one of our barn cats. The rest of the litter, had not survived, and this one, had been close to death himself. I brought him to the house, and fed him with an eye dropper. Most kittens this small, do not do well, and eventually die. This one was tough. We did not name him, for two weeks, because I figured he wouldn't make it. But he did! He was quite a funny looking little guy. His ears were too big for his body, it seemed, and his feet, he had extra toes on all four feet. His feet were huge. He was black, like his mama, but he had fine white hairs, sticking out, all over his body. He really looked strange. He also acted strange, for a kitten. We finally named him Bear Cat. He did not fear anything, or anyone. Once, when he was tiny, I put him on the floor. The dog jumped up, landed right in front of him, and woofed in his face. This little mite of fur, stood up on his hind legs, and slapped that dog on his nose! We were as surprised, as I imagine, the dog was. Phill said we should have named him, "Fearless". Phill, also said, "He's not staying in the house!" I just said, "We shall see!" He stayed. Now I was forever thankful, we saved this wonderful creature. He was not, what you would call a "lap" cat, or loving, for the most part. Bear Cat pretty much would do as he pleased. He would bite my legs, and ankles while I walked through the house. He would keep us up nights, banging cabinet doors, in the bathroom, because he wanted us, to come find him. He loved to get our feet, under the door. Some days he was a holy terror, but when Phill was having a bad time. Bear would climb up, on the bed beside him, and lay his head, on his arm. He would, lay with Phill, for as long as he needed him. He sensed when Phill, was emotional, or upset, and came on a run. Bear didn't sit in his lap, he always laid beside him. If Phill was sitting in the chair, in the bedroom, then Bear would stretch out, on the bed close to him. Phill would stroke his fur, and it gave him comfort. Sometimes, Bear, would put his feet on Phill's body, like he was letting him know, "I am here, you are not alone!" It helped calm him, to have this loving touch. Pets sense feelings, that we humans cannot. They give comfort, just by being there. It was a level of acceptance, that Phill, as a stroke survivor, never felt he received, from anyone else, myself included. I tended, to be more focused on getting through, and helping him figure out this new life. Bear Cat was just there. Day, or night, whenever he needed to feel accepted.

Chapter 47

Day 354

Easter Sunday had arrived. The weather for spring had been lousy. We could expect rain one day, and snow the next. I was ready for some sunshine. At Easter we always had ham, or pork, and summer salads. This year, at the advice of Tamy, I had the adult grandkids, bring a dish to pass. This would be the first time, they had to prepare, and bring something, to our house. Usually, I took care of it. I looked forward, to seeing how it worked.

Phill has been in pretty good spirits lately, which was wonderful! I hoped some of the emotional changes, were starting to show, some real improvement. He was always happy, to have the family around, and laughed, and joked, with some of the grandkids. It was fun to watch. Our new life has emerged, with some great perks. Phill, now, had time to spend with us, instead of always working. In past years, he would only be able to take off for a short time, to eat, then it was back to work. We all understood, we were used to it, it was our life. Now, to be able to spend the whole day together, with family was absolutely wonderful. I watched them all interact, and wondered, if they realized, how different this could have been, and how very blessed we were? This was another, one of God's gifts.

Dinner was a big success. Grandson, Ben, made deviled eggs, for the first time, and they were wonderful! Another grandson, Brian Jeffrey, tried his hand, at Au Gratin Potatoes. Britney Elizabeth, brought a dessert for us. My heart, and my stomach were full!

Chapter 48

Day 355

I woke up this morning, and both of us are sick. Phill, had put an old moldy hay bale, in the spreader to tear apart, and it didn't work, he ended up, pitching it out of the spreader, and there was a lot of moldy dust. He began, running a fever in the night. I was afraid he might be headed, into pneumonia. I, on the other hand, had a reaction, to the house being filled with smoke, from toast in the toaster. I was not running a fever. Just very congested, and wheezing pretty bad. Phill did not want to go to the doctors yet. He was struggling, with some memory issues. He had trouble remembering things, that happened only hours ago. He could not recall things, that had happened years before. Was there an issue, with his long term memory, as well? I just saw little things, that I couldn't put my finger on, that didn't seem quite right. His smile was still even. I couldn't shake the feeling, that I was missing something. I talked with Jamie, who was an ER nurse, and told her what I was seeing. She assured me, that it probably was nothing. It could be from lack of sleep, when he was sick. Not only, is he sick, but I kept him up, with my wheezing, and coughing. I tried to accept her reasoning, for what I was seeing, but was not convinced.

Day 357

I've made appointments, for both of us, with the physician's assistant, that worked with my doctor. We both were pretty sick. Phill was still, running fevers of 102, and coughing. He sounded very congested. I worried that he did, in fact have pneumonia. I coughed nonstop, at night. I began to have trouble breathing. The physician's assistant said, Phill needed an x-ray. She felt, he had early signs of pneumonia. She ordered an antibiotic for him. She decided, I had a reaction to the smoke, and ordered a steroid, plus an antibiotic. She told us, "You both are pretty sick!" I said, "Yeah, I know." We headed home to rest.

Phill woke me up in the night, in a panic, because his head hurt. Before the stroke, he never had a headache, now he got them sometimes, when he would think too much, or in this case, when he was too tired. He was upset, and scared, that he was having another stroke. I had him raise his arms, and smile for me. Everything was, as it should be. He said, his hair hurt. Maybe, I thought, some sinus congestion, was showing up, in the form of a headache. But, with some of the things that I had observed lately, it gave me, some cause for concern. I had a appointment for Mom, with our doctor, in a few days. I would discuss my concerns with her. In the meantime, I decided, to just keep an eye on him, I hoped it was, because he was sick, and nothing more. I had not, said anything to anyone, except Jamie, about the changes I had seen, in Phill. I was reluctant to cause more worry, than was necessary, at this point.

Chapter 49

Day 360

I was in the office, working this afternoon, when Young Phill came in, and closed the door. I could see worry etched, all over his face. I asked, "What's the matter?" He said, "Dad is not acting right!" I asked, "What do you mean?" He proceeded to explain, he was sitting at the kitchen table, and his dad just started starring off into space. He asked him, "Are you okay? What's the matter?" Phill replied, "I dunno!" Young Phill made a beeline for me. I felt icy fingers crawling up my spine. Those were words, so reminiscent of the conversation, between Phill, and I, the day of the stroke. I quickly headed for the house, to check on him. He seemed fine. I could see, he was tired. I sent him to rest. Young Phill, and I headed back out to the studio, to talk. I told him about my fears, and that sometimes things, didn't seem quite right. I wasn't sure, if I was just being paranoid, or if there was really an issue. I told him about the headaches, and both, short term, and long term memory problems, I had been seeing. Young Phill told me, he had noticed some things, also. Nothing, he could put his finger on directly. Maybe, there was something we were missing. Now those icy fingers wrapped themselves around my throat, and I was having trouble breathing. This was my biggest fear, to get through this last year, only to lose him? God wouldn't bring us, this far to do that, would he? I needed to get control of my anxiety, or it would upset Phill. That was not what he needed right now. He needed rest. I would talk to the doctor.

Day 363

I took Mom for her appointment, with our doctor. Everything looked good with her. That was one worry off my plate. I now took the opportunity, to talk to the doctor, about Phill. I explained, his short term seemed worse, and that now, seemed to have trouble, with long term memory as well. I told her, sometimes he really slurred words, but not all words. His balance was off, more than normal. We discussed the possibility, it could be caused, by lack of sleep, just as Jamie had suggested, or we could be dealing with something more. I worried, that he had developed a brain bleed. He was on a blood thinner, and in his seventies. He had banged his head several times lately, a couple of times, hard enough to break the skin, and make it very tender to the touch. The doctor discussed our options, with me, and she felt, an MRI would be a good idea, at this time. It would alleviate some of his anxiety, to know nothing new had occurred. I let her know I was afraid, if we told him he had to have an MRI, because of the issues he was having, it would send him into a tail spin. He would be worried to death. Instead, I asked her if it is common, to do an MRI after a year, to see the changes. She said, "Yes it is common to do an MRI, at this juncture, to see what has happened, to the brain since the stroke." I asked her, if we could tell him it was a follow up, for his one year anniversary, of his stroke. She felt this was a good idea. It was a follow up, and we could rule out any problems. I told her, I wanted to know, before we told him, if there was a problem. I needed to weigh the good, and the bad. If we had an issue that could be corrected, okay. If he was continuing to have strokes, without any way to stop them, then I wanted him to have peace. I once again felt, like someone had a hold of the rug under my feet, and was trying to pull it out from under me, and I was fighting to stay upright.

Day 364

As I laid in bed tonight, I thought back to, one year ago today. It was the last day before our lives changed. I tried to remember, how he looked, or talked, or what we did. I couldn't remember anything, about that day! How could I not remember? I began to cry. It was devastating to me, not be able to see, what he looked like, that last day. Did we do anything special? Why can't I remember? I felt, like I was experiencing the loss all over again. Phill was sound asleep beside me. I cried silently. The tears streamed over my cheeks, and on to my pillow. When I was unable to cry another tear, I contemplated the reasons why, I couldn't remember that day. I finally came to the conclusion, it was our past, not our future. Our future laid ahead, and could be as wonderful, as we wanted it to be. So what? If I didn't remember, what he looked like. I knew what he looked like now, and he was the most handsome man, in the world to me. He was the reason I got up in the morning, and the reason I kept trudging on. He was, the love of my life.

Chapter 50

Day 365

I sat in the living room, in the dark drinking my coffee, watching the fireplace. Phill was downstairs, in the basement, taking care of the woodstove. It felt so familiar. The sights, and the sounds seemed very much, like that day, one year ago. If I closed my eyes, I could almost see that day, as it unfolded. It was like, I was looking through a piece of distorted glass, each image moving, and morphing into the next, with a dreamlike quality. I saw Phill sitting across from me. I heard his speech start to change into words, that all garbled together. I could see Phill being loaded into the ambulance, and being wheeled into the ER, everyone bustling around him. The rhythmic beeping of the monitors above Phill's head, invaded my mind. I remembered him lying motionless in the bed, except for the rise, and fall of his chest. I remembered the fear. The stark white fear, of losing the one thing in the world that meant the most to me. It was hard to believe, it had been a year already. Our lives forever changed, in the blink of an eye, the beat of a heart. Look how far we had come, in this past year. When Phill first had his stroke, he lost the use of his left arm, and left leg. He had left sided neglect, couldn't feel anything, on the left. Now, he was able to move as he wanted, could see, hear, and feel on the left side. He still had to watch out, for his left arm, he wasn't always aware of where it was, but for the most part he did well. There were little changes in his behavior, that I have noticed. Some of them, warm my heart, and made me smile. I loved the way he would get in bed, from the bottom, instead of his side. He loved to lay close to me. The emphasis on words, when he speaks, was now different. He would enunciate certain words, when he wanted to drive home a point. You saw it more, when he was upset, or stressed. Before the stroke, we always kissed each other goodbye, when either one of us went anywhere. It was always a point that I insisted on. I always felt, that if anything were to happen to either one of us, I wanted the last thing, we shared to be a kiss. In the first days at home following the stroke, I would try to give Phill a kiss, and he would be either distracted, or pull away because he was trying to do something. After awhile, I gave up. In recent weeks, Phill and I, talked a lot about this past year, and the ways that things have changed. He enlightened me, to his missing those kisses. He felt, maybe, I didn't want to kiss him anymore. That filled my heart with tears. It was the furthest thing from the truth. I felt, he was rejecting me, when he pulled away. After tears on both sides, we promised to, always kiss each other goodbye. Phill still battled with his emotions, although not as much, as in the beginning. We had to consider how, and when we broke news to him. If the news was disturbing, or involved change, we had to break it to him, in the morning where he could have the day, to process the information, before bedtime. If we told him later in the day, or evening, then he is not able to process what we have told him, and he becomes upset, anxious, and unable calm down enough to sleep. I believe that with time we would see improvement. His hearing on the left, continued to be a source of difficulty, for him, especially when there was any background noise. Watching TV frustrated him, he has trouble understanding, what was being said, and what it meant. The positive changes far outweigh the negative effects, from the stroke. We survived our first year. Our future was still a blank canvas, awaiting the colors of life we choose it to be. I chose the color orange, which signified dawn to me, and a new beginning of our new life.

Today we spent the day together. I helped Phill with chores this morning. We got ready, headed for lunch, and a movie. We decided on The Olive Garden, for lunch. It was great to sit across from Phill, watch him smile and enjoy himself. I, too enjoyed myself. I don't think he really understood the significance of today, and what it meant to me, but that was okay, we were both doing, what was natural for us, finding comfort, in each other's company. We laughed all the way through "My Big Fat Greek Wedding Too", ate popcorn, and acted like a couple of kids. How good that felt. Walking around the mall, hand in hand, it almost felt like it used to, when we went out for the day. In the pet shop, we ogled the puppies, but didn't find one that appealed to us, enough to take home.

Our Lab Jake, and Mom's dog Bud, had to be put down in June. Both had been ailing. Jake hurt so much, when he would try to get up, and walk. Bud had been recently diagnosed, with end stage renal failure a few months prior. So the hard decision was made, to put them both down at the same time, and bury them side by side, forever together. All of us, Mom, Phill, and I, shed tears over the decision to let them go. Jake was my boy. He loved me as much as was possible. I named him after the song, "Feed Jake", by The Pirates Of The Mississippi. I expect he will be waiting for me, his tail wagging hard enough to shake his whole body, at the Rainbow Bridge. I was happy to know, that we would be together again, someday. Bud was my dad's dog. It was the last piece of their life together, that Mom had left. I knew it hurt to let him go. I knew he was at Dad's side, while they both, waited for Mom. I found, as I wrote this, I was just not ready, to replace Jake.

I have managed for most of the day, to keep my fears about the upcoming MRI at bay. I didn't want to think about it today. I just wanted to be, like we used to be, if only for a little while. It turned out to be a wonderful, and well deserved day!

Day 372

The volunteer at the desk led us to an office, to check in for Phill's MRI. After the paperwork was done, another person led us back to where the scan wouldbe preformed. She stopped in the hallway, pointed to a very small room with a few chairs in it, "You can wait here", she told me. I kissed Phill one last time, before he followed her down the hall, to another room. "I love you", I whispered, as he walked away. He grinned back at me, "Love you more." Wanting to be alone with my thoughts, I took the seat, furthest from the door. I didn't want to risk having to interact with someone, in the hall. I didn't know, if I could exchange trivialities right now. It was all I could do, not to let the tears, slide down my cheeks. I was terrified. With all of the changes, I had been seeing, what were the chances, it meant nothing? My hands were clammy, yet I felt, like I was freezing. I wanted this scan, but now, I was not so sure, that was is a good idea. "Please God let this be okay", I prayed. It seemed, like a long time had passed, before I saw Phill outside the room, but when I checked the time, it had only been half an hour. Was that a good sign? Or is it a bad sign? It would be at least a week, before we knew the results. That seemed like such a long time. I checked my smile, as I walked out into the hall, and said, "Hey Handsome, you ready to go?"

Day 379

My hands were clammy. I could feel my heart racing, as we sat in the office, of our doctor. I prayed, "God please make this alright." I was so scared. Sitting beside me, Phill was oblivious, of the struggle going on inside me. He was just patiently waiting. I envied his peace. The door opened, in walked the doctor. It was time to get some answers. She brought up his MRI, on the computer, and read the radiologist's report. No new injuries. It took a moment, for my mind to catch up. I repeated it to myself, "No new injuries." Praise God! The doctor then told Phill, the reason for his unsteadiness, was because he was out working those muscles, they become more fatigued, than if he was not active. If he was sitting around the house instead of working like he was, he probably wouldn't had noticed the balance issues, as much. The same with his memory, and speech. The more fatigued he became, the more pronounced these issues become. She told him to rest periodically, throughout the day. This would help recharge his batteries. The sheer relief I felt was unbelievable. As we left the office, I was so thankful. My faith was what, helped me deal, with all that had happened, this past year. I was reminded, that we serve an awesome God. Although our lives were irrevocably changed on April 9, 2015, not all of the changes were detrimental to us. We learned so many things about ourselves, and each other. We truly had weathered the storm, and survived. We were forever changed, but we were blessed. We were loved.

Phill's Thoughts

I want to add some of my thoughts, to our story. When I had the stroke, I was working twelve to fourteen hours a day, every day. It was devastating for me to lose that ability. The loss of our dairy. The herd, that Darlene, and I built over the last thirty years, took its toll on me. Through these hardships, I learned many things. One of them, how loved I was, by family, and friends. Some people, I knew only in passing, brought food to the house, for my wife, and mother-in-law, or offered help. That meant a lot to me. Our friend Merlin, dropped everything, the day of the stroke, and helped my sons, take care of our farm. That too, meant a lot.

My kids, you are never sure how much your kids have absorbed, until you face an event that changes your life. My son, Brian, took time off from his contracting jobs, to come clean, and bed the barn. Before the stroke, Young Phill, didn't seem to have a very strong interest, in the farm. He made his own little farm down the road, and seemed content with that. When I had the stroke, he stepped up, and took over the dairy, milking, and doing the chores. He ran it, like he had done it, all of his life. He told Darlene, while I was in the hospital, "I never wanted to milk cows, but I now understand why Dad loves it. These cows have personalities, and traits all their own." He was right. That is one of things, I loved most about the dairy. In this past year, we have become more of a father-son operation. We made hay together, and he has helped immeasurably with the new beef operation. I learned what my father must have felt, when I had different ideas, on how to do things. Maybe, we don't always agree, but Young Phill, stepped up when I needed him most, and that told me a lot about his character, about the man he has grown in to. Apparently, Darlene and I, did a great job raising these kids. They all stepped up, took care of their mom, and made sure she was okay.

I want to say to them, "I love each, and every one of you. I am so proud of you. Thank you, for all, that you have done." Jenny, she came almost every day to the hospital, and was there for us. Tamy, came down from Buffalo to be with us, and helped with her grandma. She also helped her mom deal with everything. Jamie, although distance separated us, was on the phone daily for moral support, and helped us understand, what was happening.

My wife. There are so many things I want to say about this woman. She is kind, and caring to everyone, not just to family and friends, but to strangers, as well. She is one of the reasons, I have come as far as I have. She is always positive, looks for the silver lining in every cloud. I knew this even, before the stroke, but now? I know each, and every day, she will do her utmost, to insure I stay focused, on getting better. I have my own personal cheerleading section. I have a very hard time talking about my love for her, without getting emotional. I cry quite often, because I can't believe, I deserve her. She however, always tells me, that she is the lucky one. That point, I'm not sure we agree on, but I know we are blessed to have each other. I call her Beautiful, she calls me Handsome. To some, that may sound corny, but to us? It is just how we see each other.

To any of you reading this, I pray you have the love of family, and friends, as I have, to help you through any dark days, you might encounter. I know it is, what has kept me going through mine.

I want to say to any of you, who had have your life turned upside down, by a stroke, don't give up. Take advantage of any rehabilitation offered, and work hard at it. Take each day as it comes, and don't worry about tomorrow.

In the United States 795,000 people will suffer a stroke this year, 20% will be caused by Atrial Fibrillation. The type of stroke my husband, Phill had. In some cases it can happen, with the first instance of A-Fib. It is a matter of life, and death that you be able to recognize the signs of a stroke. Here are some of the most important signs of a stroke.

A Sudden weakness, or numbness on one side of the body

Have them try to raise both arms. Are they able to maintain the same height on both sides?

Sudden vision changes in one, or both eyes, or difficulty swallowing

Can they see out of both eyes?

Face Drooping

Have them try to smile, both sides of the smile should be equal.

Sudden problems with balance, or walking

Is their gait normal for them? Is their balance unstable?

Slurring of words, or inability to speak,

Have the person repeat a simple sentence. Is their speech garbled, or strange?

I knew these signs, and because of that, we were able to get the medical assistance that Phill needed, in time to help stop the devastation, of the stroke. Every minute counts. Knowing these signs, can save a life, or significantly reduce the traumatic effects of a stroke, in you, or your loved one. Please remember these.

Initially this book was going to be a joint effort, for my husband Phill and I, however, he became unable to remember much from that time. The brain's way of healing I guess. So, it fell to my shoulders. This became a blessing for me. I have been able to put down on paper, all the events, and challenges, we have faced this past year. It has been extremely therapeutic. I have laughed, cried, and marveled at our perseverance, in overcoming Phill's disabilities, and rebuilding our lives. The motivation behind my writing this book, is to let other stroke survivors, and caregivers know, that you are not alone. The one resounding feeling that I experienced this past year, is that I felt alone. There are stroke groups available in many areas, if there is one near you, please take advantage of their support. I was unable to seek support, as the nearest one was sixty miles away. I also felt I would be disloyal for, "needing to seek help", in dealing with my husband. He may have felt, he was too much of a burden, if his wife had needed a support group, to deal with him. So I forged on alone. Actually, it might have been beneficial for us both, to have some support, regardless of distance. I would loved, to have had a book like this, to draw on someone else's experiences, as they navigated, through their catastrophic event. It would have validated feelings of loss, and the uncertainty this past year. I hope you can relate, and find value in our story. I hope it gives you peace.

Phill has continued, to show small signs of progress in some ways. There are still areas that are cause for concern. According to our doctor, he has the potential, to continue to improve, for up to three years. Some researchers contend; that improvement is ongoing. It is still unclear what the final toll will be in damage to his brain. Some of the deficits that he is exhibiting, have been with him, since the inception of his stroke. I feel these may be permanent, but time will tell. The brain is an amazing organ. It is able to "rewire" itself to help remember, and execute both simple, and complex tasks. Jamie explained it to her dad," Your brain is like a road map. You have always gone from point A, to point B, on a certain highway. Now that highway is gone, and you have to find a new route. Rehab helps the brain look for that new route." I found that explanation to be insightful. This was an analogy that Phill could understand.

I would like to share with you, some of the things I have learned in dealing with someone with a brain injury.

Develop a thicker skin

Many survivors have suffered an injury, that makes it impossible for them, to hear how their manner of speech, has changed. They don't realize their phrasing may come across as, abrupt, or rude. This is especially true, with the people closest to them, and their caregivers. Their level of fear, and frustration, far outweighs their ability, to control, how they voice things. Let it roll off your back. It is not important. Most times, when this occurs they are looking for comfort, and stability. Let them know you are there, for the duration. Remember that you are suffering too, and you might find, you anger more easily. If you find you need a moment, to compose yourself, walk away. It is okay to tell them they are not allowed to talk to you that way, if they become verbally abusive.

Think before you speak

You may not be dealing with the same personality, that you have dealt with before. The area affected by the injury, can alter that person's personality. How they comprehend what is being said, and how their brain processes it. You may have been able to scold that person, before their injury, and it did not have a negative effect on them, but now will cause them tremendous anxiety, and fear. Remember that how they deal with emotion, may have been altered. Stop, and think about, how what you are about to say, would affect a child. Would you say those exact words, or would you temper that phrase, so as not to cause the child to feel insecure, or stupid. I have found the way Phill's brain processes things, can be very much like a child. This does not mean, they have reverted to being a child, it means their brain, has to relearn, how to process things.

Give directions in a single sentence

This is the one I struggle with the most. I have a hard time, remembering not to give, too many directions, at once. Although it may sound simple to you, it becomes a complex task for someone with a brain injury. More than one direction at a time confuses them, and they end up forgetting what it is, that you wanted them to do. If they are complex, the brain has trouble distinguishing one, from the other, and the system becomes overloaded. In Phill's case, he becomes frustrated, and anxious. Break down the directions into a single sentence, with a single task, so they can retain it more easily, and complete the task.

Remember who you were to each other

Maybe you were once a couple in love. Now your role has changed. Take time to do something, not geared towards caretaking, or not connected to the brain injury. Maybe going to a movie, or out to dinner. Take a walk, or just sit in the park, and people watch. Remember to kiss each other, and share affection together. It is very easy for this to disappear, in the new role that you have taken on. One of the best things you can do, is laugh. Phill loves to read me funny stories, that we can laugh at. It really is, the best medicine, for what you are going through.

Be aware of how the "input" from your surroundings can lead to overload.

Everything in our world creates input. It includes sight, sound, touch, and even smell. All of these are fed into our brain, and processed. When there is an injury, both the ability to process, and the way they are processed, can be changed. In Phill's injury, certain movements, from things in his line of vision, and sounds, such as traffic would startle, and stress him, because of the way his brain tried to process this heavy input. The movement of the car itself, was input, that had to be dealt with. Expect that anything new, can cause an issue, with input for people, with a brain injury. You want them to learn to process input, but not to cause them excessive anxiety, and stress. If traffic is a problem, as with Phill, try redirecting, and giving them a task, to distract them, so they are not so focused, on the input. I had Phill look for signs for a hotel, and he was redirected. It isn't always that easy. Sometimes, they just have to struggle through, and you just have to be there for them. Loud noises seem to be a problem for Phill, and he is sensitive to smells. Both cause him anxiety. Phill can't handle television shows, that have a lot of action, or violence. They are too much input. I try to minimize the amount of stress he gets, by limiting the type of TV he watches. There is plenty of input, he has to learn to process, and I don't feel, I have to add to it, with artificial input.

Ask for help when you need it

This is the most important advice I can give you. You do not have super human strength. You do not need to face everything, alone. Ask for help. Whether it be from family, your friends, even your church. Sometimes you may need your physicians help, when dealing with the effects of a brain injury. Don't be afraid to ask! People will usually step up to the plate, and help if they have an idea, you need help. This is hard, I know from experience. It is also necessary, for you to be able to take care of this person, and yourself. If you don't take care of yourself, you won't be able to take care of them. People used to tell me, "You need to take time for yourself". I thought, "right" when am I supposed to do that? They would tell me, "go out to dinner with friends." "really?" I thought. I am supposed to leave my other half home, while I go out to dinner with our friends? How will that make him feel? Phill would have felt devastated. I could not do that. So, I appeased my soul, in other ways. I did things that I liked to do. I read, I watched TV. I called friends on the phone, and chatted. Sometimes, I took a few extra minutes when I went to the store. Sometimes, I would stop, and get a cup of coffee. They are little pieces, that help put the rest of the picture together. It helped make me whole. I can't get back what we lost, but I can adjust how I deal with it.

I hope that through my book, **<u>"A Stroke of Love"</u>,** I have been able to educate, and relate to you in some way. My goal from the start has been to help others, with what we have learned, this past year. It has been a journey filled with tragedy, and triumph. We have found unexpected blessings, in spite of the hardships. I believe that God placed us on this path to a new life, for reasons that only He knows. I know that Phill, would never had been able to stop milking cows, not because we couldn't have afforded it, but more, because he was unable to see beyond that part of his life. It is what he has always done, and even today would prefer to do. Until his stroke, I don't believe he was able to comprehend how much work, was required to maintain the dairy. Even now, he overestimates his abilities, to physically do the work, that would need to be done. God, in His infinite wisdom, took that decision, and made it for him. I believe this with all of my being. Why else, would He save him from a threat of cancer, only to strike him down with a catastrophic stroke, that according to his doctor, he should not have been able to, "walk and talk", yet battled back from? Phill is able to do much more, than they ever believed. I give the credit to God.

So we will set forth on this new journey, wherever it may lead us. I am sure there will be bumps, and pitfalls along the way, but we will make it, by placing one foot in front of the other. Steady is the course. I know that God, will be directing our steps. After all, it is His plan.

CPSIA information can be obtained
at www.ICGtesting.com
Printed in the USA
FFOW03n1814200118
44600523-44487FF